SURVIVAL ON THE BATTLEFIELD: A HANDBOOK TO MILITARY MARTIAL ARTS

BY ROBERT K. SPEAR

To my wife, Barb, for putting up with my dreams, and to my children, Pat, Shanna, Desiree, and Candice, for having to live with their fulfillment.

UNIQUE PUBLICATIONS

4201 Vanowen Place
Burbank, CA 91505

ISBN: 0-86568-093-0
Library of Congress Catalog Card Number: 87-50245

DISCLAIMER

Designer: Danilo J. Silverio
Editor: Dave Cater
Photography: Ed Ikuta

Acknowledgements

Thanks to Maj. (P) David L. Campbell for contributing the chapter, "Universal Force Dynamics in Battle Planning and Execution." His use of these theories to develop effective military strategies and tactics in map exercises at the U.S. Army's Command and General Staff College, Fort Leavenworth, Kan., was the first to prove the efficacy of this concept; to Reno at the Ramos Pawn Shop in Leavenworth, Kan., for the use of his M-1 rifle and bayonet; to Professor Don Burns, martial art coordinator for Indiana University and president of the U.S. Hapkido Federation, for his encouragement; and to Jim Channon for his graphics expertise.

About the Author

A fifth-degree black belt, Mr. Spear is considered an American pioneer in the Korean art of hapkido. He was the first American to attain a third-degree black belt in the Republic of Korea in 1975 from the Korea Hapkido Association. He is also the first American to receive a letter of certification as an instructor from that same organization. Mr. Spear is the vice chairman of the board of examiners for the United States Hapkido Federation and is a member of the Midori Yama Budokai Association.

A former army intelligence officer, Mr. Spear has taught combat fighting and self-defense to soldiers in Korea and the United States, and to civilians in Arizona, Indiana and Kansas. He is a recognized martial art theorist, and has written for several martial arts magazines. He has presented papers on the arts at the 1984 Olympic scientific Congress, the American Association for Fitness in Business, and the World Future Society.

Military tactics instructors at the U.S. Army's Command and General Staff College (CGSC) at Fort Leavenworth, Kan., have used his theories to create new tactical approaches to the modern battlefield. He has been a guest lecturer to CGSC's School for Advanced Military Sciences, and the Dallas Cowboys are teaching his theories of the dynamics of conflict to their players.

Mr. Spear holds a master's in business management from the University of Northern Colorado and a bachelor's in both music and business from Indiana University. He is currently pursuing a doctoral degree in business policy and international business at Indiana University. He is also the president and chief consultant for his business governmental consulting firm, Universal Force Dynamics, Inc. He is a member of both MENSA and INTERTEL.

Table of Contents

Introduction

Historical Background

In 1973, the U.S. Army discontinued both bayonet and hand-to-hand (combatives) training. The two reasons cited by the Army's proponent for self-defense training, the Infantry School at Fort Benning, Ga., were:

- Both the Army and the Marine Corps had experienced fatalities while conducting pugil stick training. The pugil stick was a mock rifle or a wooden quarterstaff with padding on both ends. It was used to teach bayonet fighting and aggressiveness to recruits. There were adverse congressional reactions to any military training accidents at the time, so the Army decided not to risk the possibility of any more training incidents than necessary.

- Another factor the Army considered was the need to revamp its public image after the Vietnam War. Army decisionmakers believed the technological skills of its service people should be emphasized and not their ability to kill other human beings.

What was not officially acknowledged, although it was the topic of many discussions among non-commissioned officers and officers at the grassroots level, was the inadequate practical worth of the Army's self-defense system, "Combatives." All recruits received approximately ten hours of training in boot camp on a set of techniques that were, for the most part, ineffective. The blocking system was impractical; the kicks were slow and left a person unprotected during the execution phase; the stances were awkward; and the strikes could possibly break the attacker's fingers or hands. It was commonly said they were given "Just enough skill to get themselves killed in a barroom brawl." Although there were a few good techniques, the majority were more dangerous to their users than to their antagonists.

In the early 1980s, the Army decided that bayonet training again was needed; however, Combatives were still not being taught. Although some army units trained on their own, there was still no organized, common self-defense system being taught throughout the service. Some units (particularly those in Korea and Hawaii, and the 82nd Airborne Division at Fort Bragg, N.C., encouraged tae kwon do training. The Special Forces studied Hwarang do (a legacy left by the late Michael Echanis), and the Ranger battalions used the old Combatives system. Troops at Fort Hood, Texas, were exposed to some basic Aikido training given by Sportsmind Corporation, which used both sports psychology and martial art techniques to enhance unit and individual performance.

This situation continues basically unchanged as of 1987. But that is not enough. The military needs a cohesive personal combat training system that is based upon the projected threat. It should also recognize the general level of awareness of the martial arts among troops. One recreational director at the post supporting the 9th Infantry Division estimated at least 900 soldiers in his Division were rated at the black-belt levels. This untapped reservoir of talent could easily become a core of instructors in an expanded martial arts training program for the military.

Threats of the Modern Battlefield

The threats of the modern battlefield place new requirements on troop hand-to-hand training. The military no longer has the luxury of a "front-line" mentality. For years the Army fought conventional battles from the Forward Edge of the Battle Area (FEBA) or from the Forward Line of Troops (FLOT). The front line consisted primarily of male combat-arms soldiers such as infantrymen, tankers, and artillerymen. The standard view was that only front-line combat troops should receive special training. Another common opinion was, "Why teach soldiers to fight with their hands? They're going to have their weapons (meaning rifles or pistols)." Of course one must assume the friendly forces will never run out of ammunition or be overrun by the enemy. The realities of modern combat, however, disprove these arguments.

When one considers the high probability of rear area insertions by airborne (paratroops), air mobile (heiborne), and special operations forces, the front line is no longer just "out in front," but wherever the enemy chooses to bring it. In any major battle, rear-echelon troops will be under attack around communications centers, command posts, supply depots, traffic checkpoints, and missile installations. These rear-echelon troops also have the highest percentage of female soldiers. The primary missions of these troops is to provide goods and services to the front-line combat-arms soldiers. When attacks take place in the rear areas, the enemy is said to be fighting the "deep battle," which is designed to disrupt the main battle by denying support, causing confusion and preventing reinforcements by the reserve or follow-on troops.

Training payoffs

Both front-line and rear-echelon troops (male and female) need the training to survive and repulse an enemy attack. Of course, each soldier must be given weapon-handling skills (marksmanship); however, it is also imperative that he learn how to fight hand-to-hand and with the expedient weapons, such as entrenching tools (small camp shovels), clubs, empty rifles, bayonets, and knives. A soldier's physical capabilities (strength, endurance, speed, flexibility, and balance) also are enhanced. Some psychological spin-offs include the soldier's will to close with the enemy, concentration on his battle despite outside distractions, and self-confidence. These psychological aspects are necessary for soldiers to function effectively in both weapon and hand-to-hand situations. Some older readers may remember watching newscasts of the Vietnam War showing soldiers under fire lying down and shooting anywhere but at the enemy. Some never fired their weapons at all. The noted military historian, S.L.A. Marshall, studied soldiers' performances during World War II and found that a surprising number never fired their weapons during the heat of battle. In other words, a soldier must have both *skill* and the *will to kill.*

A little needs to be said about unit cohesion (trust in, and satisfaction with your buddies) and values training. One should consider these as emotional spin-offs from martial art training. The martial arts, when properly taught, emphasize the concepts of right and wrong, ethics, and using the appropriate level of force to fit the situation. Experiments in 1982 conducted by the Army's High Technology Test Bed at Fort Lewis, Wash., determined that martial art training programs had significant impact on what the test subjects thought about their units and their fellow soldiers.

The ideal training program

Implementing service-wide training programs provide the military with a unique problem. From a huge training population, it must consider varied levels of student intelligence and prior experience within stringent time constraints. Therefore, an ideal military personnel combat system should be simple and easy to teach and learn. Soldiers wear cumbersome boots, so martial art techniques should be compatible with their attire.

A troop commander never has adequate time to train his people in every requirement; therefore, an ideal hand-to hand training system should fit into the training time that has already been allocated. Therefore, it is recommended that martial arts be incorporated into unit physical training (PT) programs.

Martial art styles

Personal battlefield combat is not like martial art tournament fighting. There are no rules, and there is usually no time to warm up or stretch prior to the engagement. One minute the soldier may be in a Command Post working as a communicator or intelligence analyst, and a moment later he may be fighting for his life against highly trained enemy soldiers.

The techniques taught to our troops, therefore, must be simple and powerful, and represent the best of several different martial art styles. One needs to understand the complexity of the martial art field to realize the difficult task facing the military.

There are well over a thousand martial art styles in the world and more are being discovered or developed constantly. However, it is still possible to categorize the various styles into three major classifications:

A. Hard styles:

These generally rely on brute force to blow through weak points of an enemy's defense. They tend to depend on the "one punch = kill philosophy. Their movements are predominantly direct or straight line (linear). They use powerful blocks that forcefully drive an attacking foot or hand off the target line. Representative styles are Korean tae kwon do and Okinawan karate.

B. Soft styles:

These are comparatively passive, and emphasize more intellectual and spiritual involvement concomitantly with their physical techniques. They are oriented more on defense and the containment or redirection of force. Their techniques involve smooth and flowing circular movements. They generally do not emphasize aggressiveness, but stress self-control. Representative styles are Japanese aikido and Chinese tai chi.

C. Integrated styles:

These combine aspects of both hard and soft styles into powerful combinations of techniques and philosophies. They tend to be situation-driven; that is, they can be passive or aggressive depending on the situation. Their philosophies lean toward ethical and expedient combat, which means matching the appropriate force and techniques to the context of the battle. This is especially useful in teaching troops moral responsibilities. For instance, if a drunken friend gets belligerent at a party and tries to choke you, his violence should be contained so neither participant sustains injuries. But if a mugger or rapist attempts to choke you in a street situation, you should feel free to neutralize the assailant as expeditiously as possible — in other words, waste him! Representative integrated styles are: Korean hapkido and hwarang do; Japanese jujitsu; Chinese wing chun, chin na, and kempo; Thai boxing; Filipino kali/arnis/escrima; and Bruce Lee's jeet kune do.

Styles can also be classified as sport vs. combat arts. Sport arts have numerous rules to lessen the chance of competition/training injuries. They emphasize the concept of fair and foul targets and techniques as opposed to the "anything-goes" attitudes found in the combat arts. Representative sports styles are: boxing, wrestling, fencing, judo, and the Japanese bamboo sword-fighting sport of kendo.

Some arts concentrate on specific primary weapons. For example, boxers use their hands, tae kwon doists use their feet, judoka throw, and escrimadores fight with rattan sticks and balisong knives. Good integrated arts such as Hapkido use everything.

This book's approach

This book, a reference manual for military martial arts, includes sections on fighting theory (the hows and whys), techniques (both simple and slightly complex), guidance for unit training managers on their training programs' structures, do-it-yourself training aids and facilities, and drills. It also addresses Soviet, North Korean, Chinese, and Middle East terrorist hand-to-hand training. It provides the theory and practical examples of how this knowledge of personal combat can be examined in higher-level contexts to teach military tactics in unit-vs-unit conflict.

Relatively inexperienced models were used throughout this book to show that the techniques are easy to understand and master. The techniques, a mixture of hapkido, jujitsu, boxing, wrestling, judo, tae kwon do, wing chun, and even some of the old Combatives moves, can be executed by males or females dressed in boots and battle-dress uniforms. They require no warm-up in a combat situation. Kicks are only below the waist, and no prodigious strength or flexibility is required (although the recommended exercises will produce them). All are intended to allow for simple, speedy execution. The training aids, facilities, and drills are products of many years of trial and error, and having to "make do" with whatever was at hand.

Ideally both the soldiers and trainers will use this handbook as a springboard to much higher levels of competence. Take what is useful, pass it on, and strive to be the best you can be. Defenders of freedom deserve to *survive on the battlefield*.

SECTION I
Tools and Techniques for Personal Combat

CHAPTER 1

Martial Art Theory

Since there are so many martial art styles that use terms endemic to their differing cultural and language backgrounds, it was important to create a common language that transcended style. It should use easy to understand Western terms.

This chapter defines a common language called Universal Force Dynamics in terms of personal combat. These terms will be used throughout to describe the combat techniques in this book.

There are only so many ways you can fold, bend, spindle, and mutilate the human body; however, you should know there are three reasons why we combat our enemy:

- To *deny* him opportunities.
- To *degrade* his techniques and defenses.
- To *disrupt* his attacks.

We accomplish these goals by using six principles or alternative courses of action when dealing with a threatening force.

Principles

Principle 1: Avoiding force

This pertains to mobility in battle. It means staying out of range or moving aside to let pass a kick, blow, or thrust. It also means ducking under a punch or jumping over a trip.

Principle 2: Leading force

This principle involves taking an opponent's attack and causing it to extend or travel further than he intended it to go. This throws him off balance, after which the defender can take control.

The defender grabs an attacker's punch.

He pulls the punching arm further than it was intended to travel, bringing the attacker off balance.

He then takes advantage of the attacker's temporary help-lessness and breaks his elbow.

Principle 3: Turning force

This principle works by changing the direction of a blow or kick, thereby taking it off line. It usually changes a linear force into a portion of a circle.

A linear kick moves toward a defender.

The kick is redirected down and to the side by a deflecting block.

The attacker's body has been turned around until his vulnerable back is exposed to a counterattack.

Principle 4: Absorbing force

An opponent's force can be absorbed until it is rendered harmless or has been exhausted. Muhammad Ali used force absorption perfectly. Whenever he faced an opponent who was known to be a strong slugger, he would cover his face and body and lay back on the ring ropes. His attacker's blows would be transmitted through Ali's arms, through his body, and into the resilient ring ropes which acted like shock absorbers. When the opponent got too tired to keep up his guard, Ali would pick him apart.

Another good example is the judo breakfalls found in Chapter 4. These dissipate the force of a fall over a wide area of the body, thereby decreasing the likelihood of an injury. We also see this principle at work with covering blocks in combat.

Principle 5: Force against force

This is the bread-and-butter of the hard arts. Two forces come together to the detriment of one. This means blowing through an opponent's defenses or hard-blocking an incoming attack. It overpowers the opponent through the superior use of strength.

Principle 6: Force harmonization

It is possible to use an opponent's force or power as your own.

The defender grabs a punch.

He uses the attacker's momentum.

And throws him to the ground.

You can also add your force to an opponent's to speed his up or force it to travel further than he would desire.

These six principles are rarely used in isolation, but rather in different combinations. For example, you can sidestep a punch (avoid), pull it as it goes by (lead and harmonize), and turn it into a throw (turn), using your opponent's momentum (harmonize).

As well as the six force principles, there are 22 dynamic factors that have impact on the use of those principles.

Dynamic factors

Factor 1: Balance

This signifies both physical and emotional balance. The idea is to maintain yours while disrupting the enemy's. You can't move effectively if you're off balance. Neither can you fight effectively if fear or anger causes you to lose control and concentration. You must maintain your physical and mental equilibrium.

Factor 2: Battle Awareness

You must stay in touch with what's going on in the fight. You should be aware of what an opponent is doing; what is happening to your front, rear, sides, and above and below you; what the terrain is like, and whether there are any obstacles that can be used. You need to use all six senses: sight, sound, touch, smell, taste and psi. These senses must be extended equally in all directions. Some martial artists call this "soft eyes." When facing an opponent, you should center your eyes on his chest. All limb and body movements are telegraphed through this area and all limbs lie within your peripheral vision. If you watch only his eyes, feet, face, or hands, he might feint with one of them and follow up from a direction that you aren't watching.

Factor 3: Cohesiveness

It helps to stick to a game plan or a fighting strategy as long as it works. Techniques and movements should support one another. For instance, if you should block a punch, the end of the blocking movement should automatically set up the start of a counterattack, which in turn sets up an opportunity to finish off your opponent. In other words, your fighting style should be logical.

Factor 4: Concentration of Power/Resources

Bringing your physical and mental attention to bear on a target involves concentrating all your force on a single point in time. Martial artists call this the "one point" or "moment." Perform a kick or a strike so the weapon travels at a relaxed pace until it explodes into the target with maximum force. This is called "snap power" and is similar to snapping a wet towel at someone in the lockerroom. The towel travels deceptively slow until the very tip of it snaps around, delivering a stinging crack at the target.

Another rule of thumb related to force concentration is to attack wide-area targets with small, narrow weapons. If you were to slap an opponent's stomach with an open hand, it would probably leave no more damage than a stinging sensation. However, if you used the ends of your stiffened fingers or a tight fist, your opponent will be bothered much more.

Factor 5: Conservation of Power/Resources

You should always conserve your energy, save a little in reserve in case a supreme effort is suddenly needed. Two essential aspects are inner calmness and a degree of self-awareness. Experienced martial artists learn to use economical movements. Often an experienced fighter in his 30s or 40s can hold his own against much younger, stronger opponents because of this factor. The older fighter must learn to garner his energy by seeking to economize his motions, and to control the situation. If the younger fighter is constantly having to react, he will eventually run out of steam. The older fighter will then have the advantage.

Factor 6: Coordination

Not only is coordination essential in the physical or athletic sense, your body and mind have to work as one. If you attempt to use a fighting technique while you are thinking that you probably won't be successful, there are better-than-ever odds that you will fail because you have not committed yourself to the action. Indecisiveness destroys an attack's or a defense's coordination and effectiveness. Remember, to harmonize with one's force, you must first be coordinated.

Factor 7: Deception

We seek to deceive our enemies by hiding our weak and strong areas and by masking our intentions. We do this by pretending to be weaker or stronger than we actually are so that we can elicit a response or attitude from our enemy. The use of feints or fakes with our head, feet, legs, hands, or body exists primarily to deceive the enemy.

Factor 8: Distance

This factor deals primarily with the range between opponents. The expression, "keeping your distance," means to keep at a range where you can effectively counter or attack your opponent while maintaining your own safety. In a personal combat situation, there are three ranges:

- *Long range* — Only long-range weapons such as kicks or leaping strikes are dangerous.
- *Midrange* — This is the maximum danger area because most weapons and defenses are within reach of one another.
- *Close range* — If you have a shorter reach than your opponent, this is the safest place other than being totally out of his range. Once you get inside his long or midrange weapons/defenses, you can use interior or close-range weapons such as head butts, elbow strikes, forearms, knees, and chokes to great effect!

Factor 9: Effort

This refers to the amount of power or speed you put into your techniques.

Factor 10: Initiative

It helps to get the drop on an opponent. As an old boxer once said, "Whoever gets there the firstest with the mostest wins." This also means to rely on your own inventiveness or judgment in absence of instructions or orders to the otherwise. It is also the willingness to take a risk.

Factor 11: Maneuver

This is the act of moving from one point to another. The object of this mobility is to catch your opponent in a disadvantageous position. You may attempt to get your opponent off balance to gain time to maneuver to a more advantageous position.

Factor 12: Momentum

This factor is neutral in nature in that it can work both to your advantage or disadvantage. Momentum is the moving inertia of maneuver. You can use momentum to maintain the initiative; however, your momentum can be used against you if you allow your opponent to throw you or to harmonize with your force.

Factor 13: Position

This is the placement of your antagonists' bodies in relation to you and others.

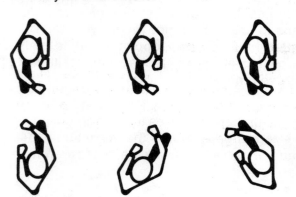

Frontal positions.   Inside positions.   Outside positions.

Being out of position means to be at an ineffective, weak, or dangerous location. (See Paul Maslak's *Strategy in Unarmed Combat,* Unique Publications, for more information on positioning).

Factor 14: Security

You must strive to keep yourself protected while fighting. If you kick, remember to position your blocking hands and arms to insure continued protection from a counterattack. Do not communicate your intentions.

Factor 15: Self-awareness

This is the ability to monitor, observe, and understand where we are in a battle and our relationship to the environment. This goes hand-in-hand with battle awareness.

Factor 16: Situation

How we react to a threat depends on the environment, the attacker, and the defender. For instance, let's say you're at a party and one of your good friends gets drunk and tries to choke you. Contain his violence without hurting him. If the situation, on the other hand, is such that you are being choked by a mugger or rapist in a street environment, more effort and lethality should be exerted.

Factor 17: Surprise

The unexpected disturbs an opponent's concentration and timing. For instance, if you spit or flick a lit cigarette into an attacker's eyes and immediately follow with a punch to his face, he will be confused and less likely to block your action.

Factor 18: Tempo

This is how you move, either fast or slow. Quickness is always a positive factor in a fight; however, sometimes a change of pace can disrupt your opponent.

Factor 19: Thinking/Acting through the objective

Never apply a blow exactly where the target exists. Always aim at a point somewhere behind it. When you strike at the target, your subconscious mind tells you to start slowing the blow before contact is made

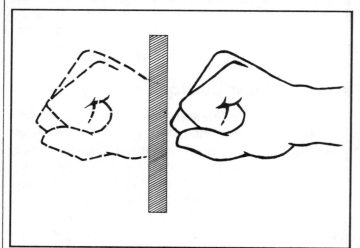

out of fear the fist might get hurt. This slows the blow and, paradoxically, actually increases the probability of self-injury because the fist slightly relaxes. If we think through a target, the blow is delivered at full force with a tight fist.

Many years ago, in a fit of rage at himself for having done something stupid, the author put his fist into a solid plaster wall. In his anger he didn't think, but reacted automatically with a tight fist traveling about 12 inches. Because he didn't dwell on the possible consequences to his hand, his form was perfect. His force projected beyond the surface of the wall and his knuckles left imprints an inch deep without any harm coming to them.

Factor 20: Timing

In any situation, timing is absolutely critical to success in the self-defense context. For example, if someone throws a punch at your face and you are late getting your block into action, you will be struck. If you are too early, you will be struck. Your timing must be exact.

Factor 22: Weapon/Force selection

The options are endless. Many books have been written detailing the many parts of the body that can be used as weapons, not to mention the hundreds of specialized and field expedient martial arts weapons close at hand. The important point to remember is that weapon and force selection are driven by the situation and your capabilities, preferences, and opportunities.

Factor 21: Vector

This is the direction a blow or movement travels and is three-dimensional in nature. Picture yourself in the center of a sphere, as opposed to a circle, and relate to vector in terms of angles to or from the center of that sphere.

CHAPTER 2

The Natural Weapons of the Body

If you must suddenly fight for your life on the battlefield, and you find yourself without weapons, don't be dismayed! The Lord has given you many parts of your body to act as powerful weapons. This chapter will illustrate the body parts and how they can be used as weapons against an opponent. None of these techniques require any special preparation, hardening, or disfigurement of your limbs. Although some karate books emphasize the use of progressive exercises designed to create callouses or bone spurs on the hands and feet to enhance them as weapons, this is not required. Hapkido Master, Ji Han Jae, was once asked what types of hand conditioning he preferred and he replied, "Gentlemen don't mutilate or deform their own bodies."

You should become familiar with the correct use of all body weapons. Once you have learned to use them, concentrate on practicing those that are the most comfortable or natural. Different body types tend to specialize in different weapon combinations. For instance, tall people tend to like long-range weapons, while shorter people usually find that the close-in, short-range weapons are ideally suited for *their* purposes.

One word of caution: Please be extremely careful when practicing with others. Some of these moves, especially those directed against hyperextended joints, can easily maim a practice buddy if too much force or a lack of common sense is applied. Treat this knowledge as you would a loaded gun. In some cases, an accident could result in the serious injury or death of a good friend.

Weapons of the Hand

The primary striking area on the front face of the fist is on the first two knuckles of the first two fingers.

This view of the back of the fist shows the top area of the first two knuckles, which is used for the backfist strike. Also shown is the bottom of the fist, which is used for the hammerfist strike.

Backfist Strike

1

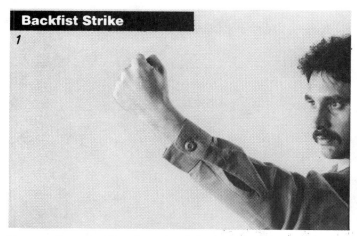

Preparatory position for a backfist to the face.

2

Execution of a backfist strike.

3

Follow-through.

Horizontal Hammerfist

1

Preparatory position for a horizontal hammerfist to the face.

2

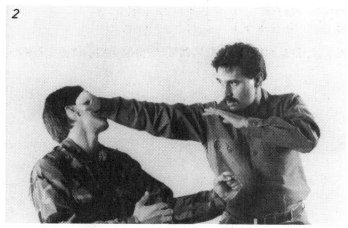

Execution of the horizontal hammerfist.

Horizontal Knife Hand

1

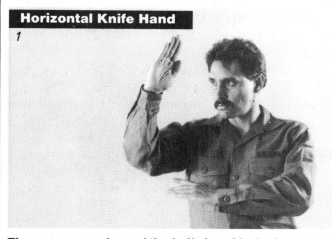

The weapon surface of the knife hand is the bottom edge.

13

2

Preparatory position for a horizontal knife hand strike to the neck.

1

The weapon surface of the ridge hand is the side of the first knuckle on the first finger. Remember to keep your thumb tucked out of the way.

3

Halfway through the horizontal knife hand movement. Note the hand turns over at the very last moment before impact. This lends snap power to the strike.

2

Preparatory position for a ridge hand strike to the neck.

4

Execution of the horizontal knife hand.

3

Halfway point, the wrist starts snapping the hand horizontally.

4

Execution of the ridge hand.

3

Execution of the palm strike breaks the jaw **and neck.** Snap power is created by keeping the wrist relaxed through- out the movement until the execution position is reached.

Palm Strike

1

Forward palm strike to the chin.

Two-finger Strike

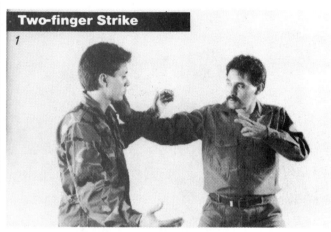

1

Two-finger strike.

2

Midpoint, showing the palm beginning to snap through.

2

Two-finger strike to the eyes.

Finger Strike

1

Supported finger strike (use against soft targets and nerve points).

2

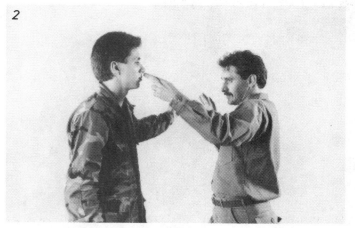

Supported finger strike to the nerve point below the septum of the nose.

Spear Hand

1

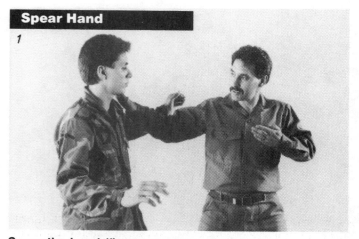

Spear the hand (fingers support each other).

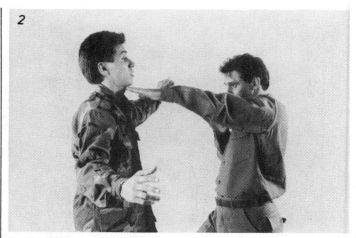

Spear hand to the throat.

Thumb Gouge

1

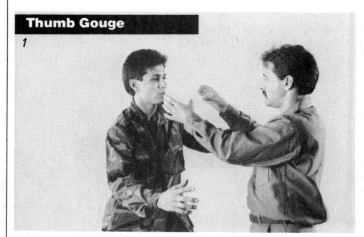

Thumb gouge.

2

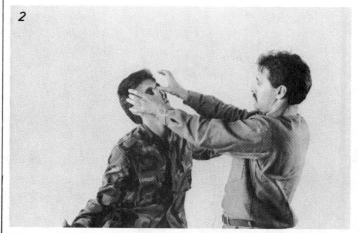

Preparatory position for the thumb gouge, the thumbs are shoved straight into the target.

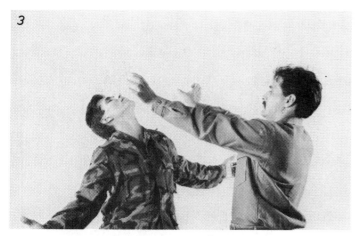

Execution. The thumbs are thrust outward.

The Claw

The claw.

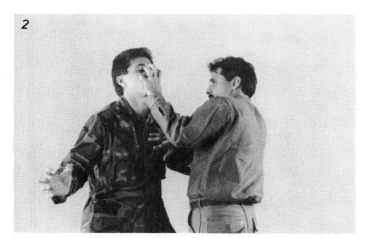

Claw to the face. This is especially effective for female soldiers with long finger nails.

Claw to the groin.

Cupped Hands

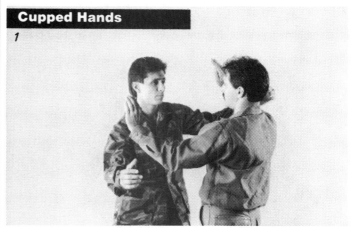

Preparatory position shows the cupped hands poised over an opponent's ears.

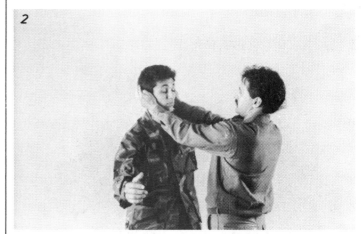

Execution. The cupped hands strike on the ear holes, creating an overpressure which breaks the ear drums and disturbs the balance of the inner ears.

Weapons of the arm

Wrist Strike

Preparatory wrist strike to the soft facial bones in **the cheek.**

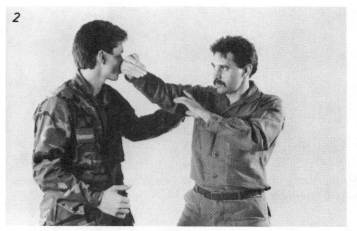

Execution requires a snap to the bent position. **The top of** the wrist is used against soft targets.

Preparatory wrist strike to the solar plexus.

Execution.

Forearm

Preparatory position for forearm to the throat. This crushes the larynx.

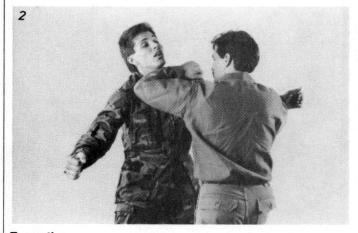

Execution.

Forearm Blow

Forearm using the protected open hand. **This adds pulling power** to the push of the forearm.

The execution crushes the chest.

Rear Elbow Strike

Preparatory position for the rear elbow strike to the body. Note that the hand is wide open to allow for **coordination** between the pulling and pushing muscles of the arm.

Execution.

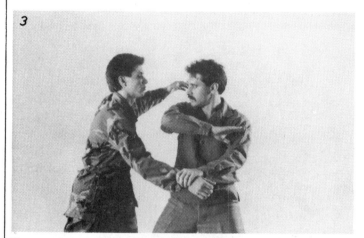

Preparatory position for an elbow strike to the throat.

Execution.

1

The stiffened arm can be used like a clothesline. This is seen in football (as a foul) and in professional wrestling. When used against the throat, it can be deadly.

2

The opponents come together.

3

Execution.

Weapons of the feet

The pointed toes are excellent weapons when they are protected by boots or shoes. Here, the pointed toes attack the groin.

Knife edge of the foot to the shin.

Inside foot to the shin. The inner edge of the foot can be effective, but it is awkward to get accustomed to.

Both the heel bottom and the ball can be used. The bottom of the heel is stomped to the face.

The ball of the heel is driven into the hamstring and rear knee area.

Weapons of the leg

Knee to the groin.

Knee to the face.

The rear of the hips can be used to strike the groin.

Weapons of the head

The forehead, back and side of the head can be used against the face.

Vital points

The vulnerabilities of the human body are many and complex. The following pictures show a few of the several hundred vital points that are considered higher payoff targets. Memorize these and pinpoint them on a partner's body.

Front view of body vital points

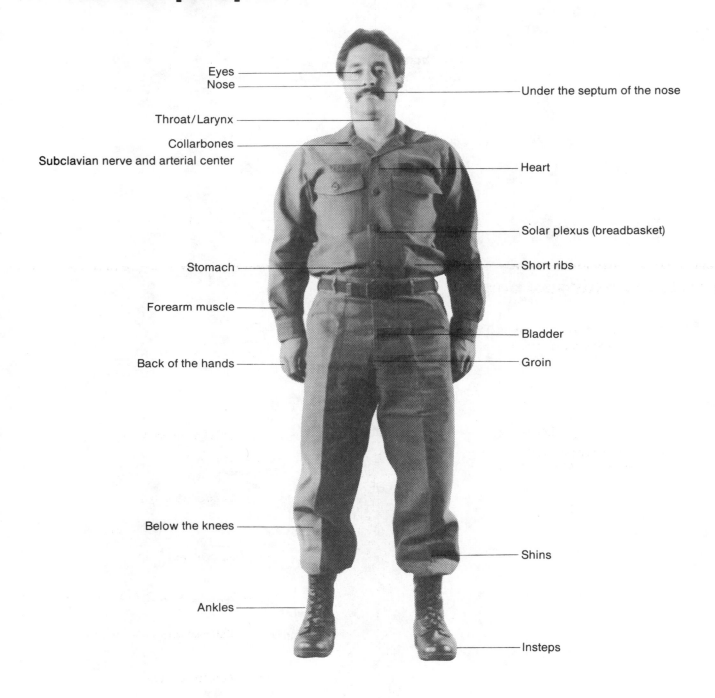

Eyes
Nose
Throat/Larynx
Collarbones
Subclavian nerve and arterial center
Stomach
Forearm muscle
Back of the hands
Below the knees
Ankles

Under the septum of the nose
Heart
Solar plexus (breadbasket)
Short ribs
Bladder
Groin
Shins
Insteps

Side view of body vital points

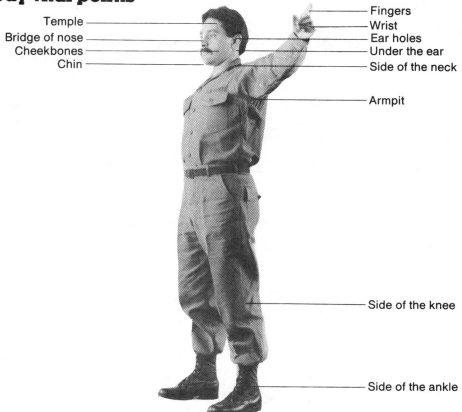

Temple — Fingers
Bridge of nose — Wrist
Cheekbones — Ear holes
Chin — Under the ear
— Side of the neck

— Armpit

— Side of the knee

— Side of the ankle

Rear view of body vital points

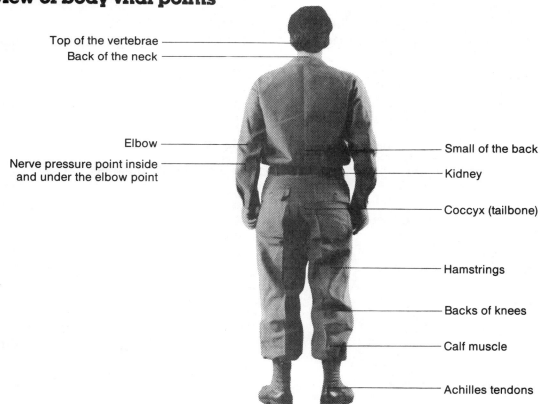

Top of the vertebrae —
Back of the neck —

Elbow — — Small of the back

Nerve pressure point inside
and under the elbow point — — Kidney

— Coccyx (tailbone)

— Hamstrings

— Backs of knees

— Calf muscle

— Achilles tendons

Recommended targets

The following matrix gives the preferred or high payoff targets for each body weapon and the probable results.

Weapon	Targets	Results
Fist	Eyes	Temporary blindness, watering
	Nose	Shock, impaired breathing, bleeding
	Chin (never hit mouth directly, teeth cut)	Unconsciousness, teeth and tongue damage
	Throat	Death from strangulation
	Solar plexus	Arrests breathing temporarily
	Armpit	Temporary numbing of arm
	Short ribs	Pain, arrests breathing
	Kidney	Pain, shock, internal bleeding
	Groin	Pain, shock, incapacitation
Backfist	Cheek bones	Pain to facial nerves affects eyes
	Nose	Bleeding, shock, impaired breathing
	Short ribs	Pain, bends opponent over
Hammerfist	Nose	Pain, bleeding, shock, impaired breathing
	Cheek bones	Pain to facial nerves
	Collarbones	Broken bone/incapacitated arm, nausea
	Forearm nerve point	Grip release
	Calf or ankle (when blocking a kick)	Intense pain, cramping
Knife hand	Throat	Death by strangulation
	Side of neck just under the ear	Possible death, unconsciousness
	Side of neck over the carotid region	Stun, possible unconsciousness
	Back of neck at top of vertebrae	Possible death, unconsciousness
	Inner side of wrist	Release of grip
	Collarbone	Incapacitation of the arm, nausea
Ridge hand	Bridge over nose	Stun
	Under the septum	Intense, eye-watering pain
	Throat	Death by strangulation
	Groin	Pain, shock, incapacitation
Palm strike	Under the tip of the nose	Intense pain, bleeding, impaired breathing
	Up under the chin	Unconsciousness, broken jaw, possible broken neck
	Top vertebrae in back of neck	Unconsciousness
	Heart	Stun, disrupted breathing
	Solar plexus	Arrested breathing
	Bladder	Possible long-term death because of internal infection
	Kidneys	Shock, internal bleeding
Two-finger strike	Eyes	Blindness, temporary
Supported finger strike	Eyes	Blindness, death if driven through eye sockets into brain
	Septum under the nose	Intense pain
	Throat	Choking

Continued...

Weapon	Targets	Results
Thumb gouge	Eyes	Blindness, shock
	Nerve centers	Pain, numbness, weakness in area
Claw	Eyes	Temporary blindness
	Face	Pain and bleeding
	Stomach	Pain and shock, disrupts internal energy flow
	Groin	Pain and incapacitation
	Subclavian/collarbone area	Intense pain
Cupped hands	Ear holes	Broken eardrums, disorientation
Wrist strike	Cheek bones	Pain to facial nerves
	Throat	Choking
	Solar plexus	Arrested breathing
	Short ribs	Disrupted breathing, pain
	Inner wrist	Blocked punch
	Underneath forearm	Blocked punch or grab
Forearm	Throat	Death by strangulation
	Ribs	Intense pain, possible internal bleeding
	Limbs	Blocked strikes and kicks
	Elbows	Incapacitated arm, nausea, shock
Elbow	Solar plexus	Arrested breathing
	Temples	Unconsciousness, possible death
	Chin	Unconsciousness, broken jaw and teeth
	Throat	Death by strangulation
Closeline	Throat	Choking, knocked to ground
	Nose	Pain, bleeding, impaired breathing
Pointed toes	Groin	Incapacitation, shock, pain
	Leg muscles	Cramps
	Head (when opponent is on ground)	Unconsciousness
Foot's knife edge	Shin	Intense pain, broken leg
	Knees (back, front, or sides)	Broken leg, torn tendons, dislocated knees, nausea
	Stomach	Arrested breathing, possible internal injuries
Foot's inner edge	Shin	Intense pain, broken leg
	Knee	Dislocated knee, nausea, pain
	Ankle	Broken ankle, nausea, pain
	Achilles Tendon	Incapacitation, nausea
Foot's instep	Knee (side or back)	Dislocated knee, intense nerve numbing
	Groin	Incapacitation
Bottom of heel	Face	Shock, bleeding, unconsciousness
	Groin	Incapacitation
	Knee	Dislocated knee, nausea, pain
	Instep	Broken foot, nausea, intense pain
Ball of heel	Hamstrings	Charlie horse and cramps, slowed movements
	Calves	Charlie horse and cramps, slowed movements
	Spine	Pain, possible paralysis
	Kidneys	Shock, possible internal bleeding

Continued . . .

Weapon	Targets	Results
Knee	Groin	Incapacitation
	Face	Shock, bleeding, disorientation
	Solar plexus	Arrested breathing
Hip	Groin	Stun, disrupt breathing
Head	Face	Stun

CHAPTER 3

Kicks

Leg muscles are larger, longer, and more powerful than the arm's. They are, therefore, able to deliver far more force. Although kicking is a time-honored tradition in many Oriental martial arts, it has only recently become acceptable in Western fighting. Even though kicking was used in the Greek pankration arts and in French savate, most other Western societies believed it to be an "unfair" practice. On the battlefield and in the street, there is no such thing as fair or foul — anything goes. Because kicks are so powerful (thereby producing more damage) and because they can be very useful on the battlefield, the most effective and easiest ones have been selected for this chapter.

Kicks should be executed with as much snap power as possible. The secret is doing them with a fairly relaxed leg. Most beginning martial artists try too hard, which causes muscle tension, which is self-defeating because it takes away the very power students are attempting to develop. Once the movement becomes familiar to the student, the leg will start to loosen up. As with most fighting techniques, mastery does not happen overnight. Keep practicing these kicks until you can do them with force from any position and from any angle.

One more word about snap power: The foot should move through its motion in a fairly relaxed manner until it has almost reached its target. At that time it should explode suddenly into the target, instantly releasing its kinetic energy. This snapping power performs two functions: it greatly increases the force of the kick, and it helps throw off the timing of an opponent's blocks and counters. To execute a good, snappy kick you must be limber and concentrate on following through. Can you imagine a golfer or a batter trying to stop his swing at the point of contact with the ball? Of course not. They carry their swings through and around.

The following nine kicks are taken primarily from the arts of hapkido and hwarang do. They were selected because they don't require limbering exercises prior to their use in combat. They are kept low to reduce the danger of counterattacks and to increase the probability of success.

The front snap kick

Starting position, the kicking foot is to the rear.

Bring the knee up and point it toward the target.

Extend the leg, thrust the hips forward, and snap the pointed toes into the target.

Quickly retrieve your foot.

Return to the starting position.

Low side kick

Starting position, the kicking foot is to the rear.

The knee is chambered (bent) across the body.

The foot's knife edge is snapped into the target knee.

The foot is retrieved to the chambered position.

Return to the starting position.

Midpoint side kick

Starting position.

Chamber the knee higher and to the front toward the target.

Extend the knife edge of the foot into the opponent's stomach.

Retrieve your leg to the chambered position.

Return to the starting position.

Back side kick

Start facing away from your opponent.

Chamber your knee forward, looking for the target over your shoulder.

Extend the heel backward while watching the target under your arm.

Return to the start while maintaining surveillance.

Shinbone kick

Starting position.

Chamber the knee back and to the outside.

Snap the foot through in an arc, striking the shin with the inner edge of your foot.

Return to the start.

Hamstring kick

Low roundhouse kick

Starting position.

Start.

Raise your knee and foot high to the outside and forward.

Chamber your knee to the outside.

Swing the ball of your heel at a 45-degree angle across and down behind your opponent's leg into his hamstring tendon. This is a great technique to use in a clinch situation.

Snap your instep into his side knee and return to the start.

Heel stomp

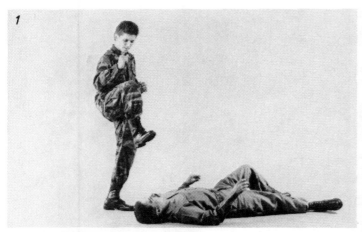

Chamber the leg over the target.

Stomp the heel into the target.

Heel thrust kick to the knee

Start.

Chamber the knee a little lower this time.

Thrust the heel into the knee and retrieve.

The above kicks are generally used in combination and with strikes. For instance, the midpoint side kick may be followed by a back side kick.

CHAPTER 4

Breakfalls

One of the more important skills to be gained from martial arts training is learning to fall safely. The breakfall system presented in this chapter is the same used in judo and hapkido. Although the system used in aikido is effective, its more rolling movements tend to place too much stress on the knees and ankles.

The natural instinct when falling is to catch ourselves by sticking out a hand or arm. Unfortunately, your body weight and inertia are concentrated on the hand or arm at the moment of impact. This may produce a sprain, or a broken wrist or elbow, dislocated shoulder, or broken collarbone. The best way to break a fall is to distribute the impact's force over a wide area of the body. The following exercises are designed to gradually develop your skill and self-confidence so you can safely take a fall from a full-force throw. No throws should be attempted until everyone involved has learned how to fall correctly.

Sitting backfall

Starting position is seated with arms crossed over your chest and your chin tucked into your chest.

Throw yourself backward, keep your chin tucked and begin to uncross your arms.

Keeping your chin tucked, snap your arms out and down at a 45-degree angle to each side and slap the ground hard as your back makes contact.

Squatting backfall (attempt only when the sitting backfall is mastered)

Squat to start.

Roll backward.

Hit the ground. Remember to keep the chin tucked to prevent banging your head on the ground.

Standing backfall

Start standing up.

Roll back (or throw yourself back when you are confident).

Hit the ground with a slap.

Side breakfalls

Start out lying on your left hip/side, left arm extended at a 45-degree angle, and with your chin tucked in.

Roll up onto your shoulders, throwing yourself over to the other side.

Land on your right side, slapping with your right hand. Don't let your legs cross or your knees hit. Alternate from side to side.

Squatting sidefall

1

Squat to start.

2

Extend your right leg to the front and fall.

3

Land on your left side, slapping out. Repeat to the other side.

Standing sidefall

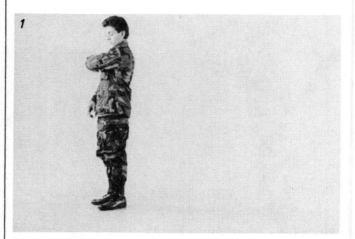

1

Start standing up.

2

Sweep up you left foot and fall down to the left.

3

Land on your left side, slapping out. Repeat to the right.

Forward roll to a sidefall

1

Step forward on your right foot and extend your right arm up and slightly bent (keeping your head inside the resulting circle of the arm). Place your left hand on the ground with its hand turned back toward the rear.

2

Roll straight forward.

3

Land on your left side and slap out with your left hand. Repeat to the other side. Eventually, this can be executed without the step-by-step roll by throwing yourself through and flipping forward to land on your side. This can be made more challenging by running and diving over several people on their hands and knees while flipping into the roll and breaking the fall at the last second.

Standing frontfall

1

From a starting position...

2

Let yourself fall straight forward and...

3

Slap your hands and forearms onto the mat.

Practice these falling techniques until they become automatic. The instinct to reach out to catch yourself must be completely overridden. Practice sessions with 30-50 repetitions of basic and advanced falls is encouraged. Breaking these falls instinctively could someday save your life. It will surely help minimize serious training accidents.

CHAPTER 5

Throws

Violently throwing an opponent to the ground is effective in rendering him combat ineffective. Some of the following throws are used in judo or wrestling; however, the joint-breaking examples come from hap-kido, hwarang do, and jujitsu. Throws primarily use the force principles of leading, turning, and harmonization. You must lead your opponent off balance, turn his vector or direction of movement into a circle, and harmonize your force with his momentum. Remember to maintain a hold on your opponent after he lands so you maintain control. Finish him off with a strike, kick, or joint break. Although there are close to 100 throws, only six of the more effective ones are presented in this chapter.

Hip throw

Pull your opponent toward you to break his balance.

Slip your arm around his arm and step across his body.

Squat slightly, lift his waist and pull his arm around to your front.

As he starts moving forward, straighten your legs, bend, and pull his waist and arm around your body.

As he falls, maintain your grip on his arm.

Shoulder throw

Pull his arm toward you.

Step across his body, turning your back to him, while placing your shoulder under his arm pit and clamping his arm to you with your free arm. Squat slightly.

Lever his arm and your upper body forward and down while straightening your legs.

Maintain control as he falls.

Back trip

Grab you opponent's jacket front (or neck) and his wrist, pulling him toward you.

Step forward until you are even with his body.

Raise your inside leg behind him and...

Sweep it back through against his leg(s). Pull his arm and push his chest.

Maintain control as he falls.

Monkey roll

If your opponent rushes or pushes you, grab his jacket front (or ears, head, or hair), and...

Shoot down between his legs while placing one or both feet in his stomach or groin.

Pull him down to you while you extend your leg(s).

As he falls on his back, maintain your grip...

And your momentum so you follow him on over to land on his chest.

Finish him off while his breath is knocked out.

Hip throw with an elbow break

1

Grab your opponent's opposite wrist and pull him toward you.

2

Step across his body, slip your arm around his waist and **shoot** your hips in front of him.

3

Use his hyperextended arm as a lever to force him over the throw. This will break his elbow and change the angle of his fall so he lands on his face or head.

Arm throw with an elbow break

1

Grab and pull his opposite wrist.

2

Pivot under his arm, keeping his wrist turned upward. Grab his upper arm to stabilize it and lever his wrist down while throwing him over your shoulder. This breaks his elbow while it throws him on his head.

45

CHAPTER 6

Chokes, Locks, and Come-Alongs

Chokes are used to kill or render an opponent unconscious. Joint locks stabilize an opponent or produce an injury with high shock value. Come-alongs control and move prisoners. Again, there are several hundred possible techniques within these categories. A few tried and proven techniques from hapkido, jujitsu, combatives, wrestling and judo have been selected.

Rear chokes

Bar arm choke from the rear

Encircle your opponent's throat from behind with your forearm. Grab your upper arm.

Lower your held arm behind his head and grasp your other arm. Squeeze your arms together. This will cut off his air supply.

Bar arm with neck break

This is identical to the choke except the non-barring arm reaches over and wrenches the side of the opponent's head into a neck break.

Front Chokes

Crossed-hands choke

1

Cross your wrists and insert your thumbs...

2

Deeply under your opponent's collar.

3

Uncross your hands. This causes the knife edges of your hands to press harshly against the side of his neck, thereby cutting off both his air supply and blood flow to his brain.

Bar arm choke from the front

1

Place your forearm into your opponent's throat and encircle his neck with your other arm.

2

Grab your bar arm and squeeze. This will cut off his air supply.

Locks and come-alongs

Full nelson

This is a stabilization technique. Reach under your opponent's arms and lace your fingers behind his neck, pressing his head down.

Modified full nelson

This version is much more painful and more difficult from which to escape. Instead of going behind your opponent's head, claw into the subclavian area and grasp his collarbone. The pain is excruciating.

Devil's handshake

Clasp your opponent's hand as if shaking hands.

Quickly turn his wrist upward while raising his arm and reach underneath his elbow for his opposite shoulder.

Lever his forearm down, hyperextending his elbow joint while pushing his fingers back toward him. This is an excellent come-along.

Elbow break

Grab your opponent's wrist and pull his arm straight. Place the part of your forearm closest to *your* elbow against his arm immediately above *his* elbow joint. Open your hand to harden your arm. If your placement action is done as a blow, it will break his elbow and cause him great pain and shock. If you are more gentle, this becomes a hold-down by pressing him down to the ground. Be careful in practice; it only takes seven-to-ten pounds of pressure to break a hyperextended elbow.

Front elbow lock

1

Swing your arm in a very large circle up and around his arm. This works well in defending a shoulder grab or in blocking a haymaker punch.

2

Circling his arm will trap his wrist under your armpit.

3

Reach over and place your free hand on his shoulder and grab your free hand's forearm with your trapping hand.

4

Arch both wrists, putting stress on his hyperextended elbow. Take him anywhere you want him to go.

Shoulder to elbow break

1

Grab your opponent's wrist with both hands and...

2

Pivot, lunging your shoulder into his hyperextended elbow and thereby breaking it.

Side elbow lock come-along

1

2

3

Clasp and maintain a handshake grip while you reach over his arm and circle under his elbow until you can grasp your wrist. Note the strain this puts on both his wrist and elbow.

Side wrist come-along

From the side of your opponent, reach under his elbow and grab his fingers and hand. Add your outside hand and pull backward on his hand while keeping his elbow bent.

Hammer lock — The wrong way

Hammer lock — The right way

Bending his hand into a wrist lock while forcing his arm up is a good come-along, except your face may be left unprotected from a backward fist.

Once the hammer lock is applied, tuck your face down against his back, thereby preventing a backfist counter.

Side headlock

Place your opponent's head and neck into the crook of your arm from the side and squeeze.

Don't stand there squeezing, hoping for a submission. This is not a wrestling match! Lean back into the lock and kick up your feet.

If you're holding tightly, your subsequent fall may break his neck.

Front headlock

Encircle your opponent's head and throat from above, clasp your hands and squeeze.

Throw your feet back...

And land on his head with your full body weight.

55

CHAPTER 7

Defenses Against Punches and Strikes

Before getting very deeply into this chapter, you may want to review the theory material in Chapter 1. Defenses against punch attacks require a thorough understanding of the dynamics of force.

The martial arts features many excellent blocking systems. All have strong and weak aspects. The system presented here is designed to use some of the more effective techniques found in boxing, hapkido, tae kwon do, karate, and wing chun. The key is that if an attempt to block a punch is unsuccessful, minimal danger or damage will result. Therefore, hard blocks that carry beyond the line of attack were rejected. Correct timing is paramount. If you block at the right moment, you'll have no problem. If your block is early and it carries beyond the line of attack, you'll be open to attack. Of course, if you're late with any block, you're probably going to get nailed. Covering and deflection blocks, based upon the principles of absorption and turning, provide security and lessen the importance of timing.

You'll also see examples of circular blocks because they fit the above criteria. Some blocks are designed only to protect while others set up devastating counterattacks. Many Westerners are more accustomed to blocking with one arm and countering with the other. Certain Chinese systems, such as wing chun, use the blocking arm to counterattack. This gives the defender time and the element of surprise. If you would like to learn more about the hundreds of aspects of blocking, read Paul Maslak's two volumes on unarmed combat strategy, *Strategy In Unarmed Combat* and *What The Masters Know*, published by Unique Publications.

The stance is a key aspect in effective blocking. Many arts teach classic stances based upon animal movements. For instance, there is the horse stance, the cat stance, and the crane stance. Unfortunately they can be difficult to master and tend to support only those fighting systems from which they are taken. For military training purposes, stances must be easy to learn, comfortable, versatile, stable, and provide protection or security. The following pictures show some stances with their trade-offs.

Boxer's stance

Although the boxer's stance is comfortable, it does not provide adequate low-line protection.

Hapkido fighting stance

This stance provides high-line protection with the vertical arm to the front and low-line protection with the horizontal arm. Your weight should be evenly distributed over both feet and your groin should be turned away more than it is in the boxer's stance.

Modified cat stance

Although this stance seems similar to the hapkido stance, it differs in that most of your weight should be over your rear foot. This provides protection to your front knee and leg by allowing them to give if they are kicked. The trade-off is less mobility to the rear.

Hand positions

It is OK to hold your hands in a fist or leave them open. Fists are good for some of the force-against-force types of blocks and punching attacks and counterattacks. Open hands are good for covering types of blocks, entrapments, and open-hand attacks and counters.

Economical blocking movements

A block need travel only as far as absolutely necessary to accomplish its task of protection unless it is being turned into a counterattack. In this case, it travels from an on-guard position to...

The blocking position.

Deflection blocks

An attacker's blow is deflected to...

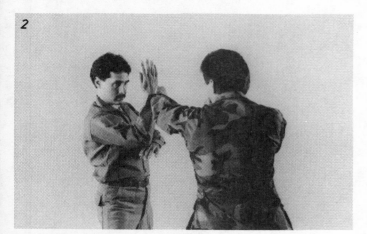

The inside.

Now a blow is deflected to...

The outside. Note these blocks do not chase after the blow once it has passed.

Now let's look at some specific blocks for several different threats:

Arm dislocate

Many blows can be taught as they come in. Here the defender...

Changes the attacker's linear punch into a circle by catching the attacking wrist and bringing it across his body as he pivots.

Once the circle reaches its highest point...

The defender pulls straight down to dislocate the attacker's elbow and shoulder.

Tendon tear

As the attacker punches, the defender catches his wrist in his own crossed wrists.

The defender drops his inside hand down to grasp the heel of the attacker's hand.

With a fluid motion, the defender pivots...

Under the attacker's arm and...

Pulls downward quickly and strongly. This rips out the attacker's forearm tendon and breaks his wrist. Note the defender's feet position showing the pivot ending at the side of the attacker.

Sticky hand block with same side hand

As the attacker jabs, the defender brings his hand down on top of the punching hand. This forces it off the target line.

As the attacker begins to withdraw, the defender's hand sticks like flypaper and then uses the attacker's withdrawing motion to...

Suddenly counterjab into the attacker's face. This sequence happens very quickly. It is an excellent technique to use against boxers because they are not used to such movements. Sticky hands are common to wing chun, hapkido and hwarang do.

Elbow break

As the attacker punches...

Step outside and catch his wrist as it goes by. Aim your grasp at his forearm so by the time it closes, it will be on the wrist.

Pull his arm straight and slam your forearm into the hyperextended elbow.

Avoid Counterstrike

The defender steps 45 degrees forward and to the outside to avoid the punch while pushing slightly on the attacker's arm to the inside and down.

While the attacker's momentum carries him forward, the defender counters with a ridge hand strike to just under the septum area of the nose.

If you push up on the attacking arm, you can...

Punch into the armpit's nerve center or...

Into his shortribs.

Deflected body punch with counter

As the attacker begins a body punch...

Deflect it with your forearm.

Uppercut jam

As the attacker prepares to uppercut with his left hand...

Jam it with your forearm.

Backfist block

As the attacker begins a backfist strike...

Bring up an open hand to act as an absorption block.

CHAPTER 8

Unarmed Defenses Against Club Attacks

During the heat of battle, after the bullets are spent, there is a great likelihood of being clubbed to death. Whether it is a stick, an empty rifle, or an entrenching tool, there is always a plentitude of available clubs. Remember, regardless of the club, the same self-defense theories can be applied.

The scissors block

As the attacker prepares to swing a forehand strike...

Quickly step forward and bring your left arm forward and down against his wrist while you bring your right arm up against the underside of his upper arm in a scissoring motion.

This will shatter the attacker's elbow.

Backhand elbow break

1

The attacker prepares to swing backhandedly into your face.

2

Quickly step forward and catch his wrist.

3

Continue to pivot, bringing the attacker's arm over your shoulder and pulling down to break his elbow.

Baseball bat forearm jam

1

The attacker prepares a forehand swing with a two-handed baseball bat grip.

2

Step inside and jam your forearms against his and...

3

Follow up with a knee kick.

67

Rush and tackle

When you see that your attacker is about to swing his club...

Sway your body back out of the way.

As the club passes by, come forward and...

Tackle him around the body before he can reverse his swing. Note that proper timing is critical for this technique.

Hugging throw

As the attacker winds up with both hands...

Rush in. Hug both your arms around the attacker's.

Pivot, using his momentum and his own power, and throw him around and down.

CHAPTER 9

Unarmed Defenses Against Knife Attacks

Many fear facing a knife-wielding opponent. The thought of cold steel violating our bodies is rather chilling. In fact, one of the worst dangers is allowing a knife to become a psychological weapon. If you let your mind dwell too much on the possible outcomes, you may tend to freeze. This would allow the very worst of expectations, since your movement would be restricted.

To overcome this psychological disadvantage, develop an aggressive, positive attitude. Tell yourself you will try not to get cut or stabbed. If you are harmed, you must vow to make him pay tenfold for every hurt he inflicts upon you. The late fighter and actor, Bruce Lee, once said, "Forget about winning and losing; forget about pride and pain. Let your opponent graze your skin and you smash into his flesh; let him smash into your flesh and you fracture his bones; let him fracture your bones and you take his life! Do not be concerned with you escaping safely — lay your life before him!"

In other words, your most dangerous enemy is yourself and your lack of self-confidence. In the heat of battle, wounds are seldom as painful as you might expect. The combination of adrenaline (the body's natural "upper" chemical) and endorphins (the body's natural painkillers) will minimize the impact of superficial wounds. This chemical defense mechanism will increase your probability to function and survive even if severely wounded. Remember, *make him pay the ultimate price.*

Once you have removed the psychological block, you will see that the methods for dealing with a knife attack are the same in theory as those used against a club or fist. The only differences are the higher level of lethality and the smaller margin for error. Let's look at several typical situations and available options for neutralizing these attacks. These techniques are taken primarily from hapkido and hwarang do.

Shoulder throw

As the attacker prepares to slash with a forehand...

Block his arm...

Trapping it.

Quickly step in, pull, and...

Execute a shoulder throw.

Scissors block of a forehand slash

As the attacker slashes down and across...

Execute a scissors block to break his elbow.

Hand kick

If the attacker is foolish enough to hold his knife...

Out in front of his body, you may...

Have an opportunity to front snap kick the knife out of his hand. It is recommended that you use a wooden practice knife to learn since there is little control of where the knife will come down.

Back slash elbow break

As the attacker commences a backhand slash...

Step in to catch his wrist.

Then execute a forearm...

Elbow break.

Outside lockout

The attacker begins to thrust forward.

Step outside the line of the thrust and block his wrist with...

Interlocked thumbs. (Here we see the correct interlock position).

Hold onto his wrist and pivot under his arm.

Continue to turn into him and pull down on the elbow lock...

Putting strain on his shoulder, elbow and back.

"Suicide" counter

As the attacker thrusts...

Step to the inside and block his wrist outward.

Pivot under his arm...

Pull back on his knife hand and...

Plant the knife in his stomach.

Overhead counter-A

1

The attacker prepares to come straight down with an overhead stab.

2

Lunge forward and to his outside, catching the descending knife arm with your outside hand before he has a chance to gain too much momentum.

3

Bring your inside hand up behind his arm and lever the knife hand backward. (The author once saw this technique used in a street fight and watched the attacker's knife fly 30 feet to the rear while the attacker was still on the way down).

Overhead counter-B

1

Similar in concept to the "suicide" counter of a thrust, we see a step to the outside...

2

And a grab of the top of the knife hand as it passes by to...

3

Force the attacker's hand further than he intended it to go (leading his force), into his own groin.

Floor defense

The attacker prepares to plunge his knife downward into your chest.

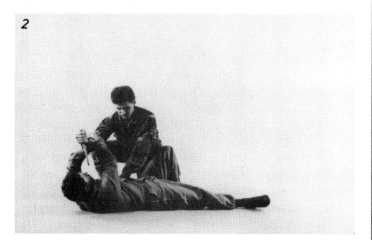

Reach up to...

Block the descending forearm and reach over the...

Elbow and pull down and across your body to break his elbow and pull his off yours.

Practice

Use wooden knives to prevent accidents.

77

CHAPTER 10

Unarmed Defenses Against Bayonet Attacks

We're almost out of ammunition and we're getting ready to counterattack. "Fix bayonets," says the captain. "Nothing strikes fear in the hearts of the enemy like cold steel!"

Maybe that's true if you don't know how to defend yourself; however, the bayonet mounted on a rifle is a rather awkward weapon. If you know what you're doing, you cannot only defend yourself against the bayonet, you can take the rifle out of an opponent's hands. How? Let's take a look at the purpose of the rifle/bayonet combination.

In the past, the bayonet was mounted on the single-shot musket to provide a spear or pike as a secondary or backup weapon. It was used as one element in a "wall of steel" formed by soldiers advancing or holding their ranks. It was never designed as a stand-alone weapon. For one thing, the weapon's balance does not allow for ease of handling. With the demise of rank-ordered, large-scale unit combat after the Civil War, the usefulness of the bayonet diminished. This is especially true today with the use of lightweight assault rifles such as the American M-16 and the Soviet AK-47. Both are designed primarily to put out a high rate of fire. They are not very suitable as bludgeons or clubs. Because they are relatively short, they don't provide the long reach found in the classic M-1 rifle used in this chapter.

In any case, you *can* defeat an opponent and his bayonet with your bare hands! The following illustrations show how (for training safety, practice with the scabbard on the bayonet).

Short lunge defense

Stand in an on-guard position when the attacker prepares to thrust.

Step outside the line of the thrust and grab the rifle barrel as it passes by. Pull on the rifle to lead his force.

Maintain your hold on the barrel while you shove it up. Step in to grab the rifle stock.

Continue to push and pull the rifle in a circle while the attacker is off balance.

As the circle is completed, pull the rifle away and prepare to execute a short thrust of your own.

Charging lunge defense

1

The attacker prepares to charge.

2

Step to the outside.

3

Bring your forearm across in a deflecting block as you step to the outside and turn your body sideways.

4

After the deflection, continue to bring your arm across your body in a wind-up while the attacker's momentum carries him forward.

5

Unleash an elbow strike into his face as he passes by.

Slash defense

The attacker prepares to slash.

Quickly step inside the line of the descending bayonet and raise your arm to block and then catch the rifle barrel.

Grab the stock and...

Execute a take-away and a . . .

Short thrust counter.

Horizontal butt stroke defense | Vertical butt stroke defense

The attacker prepares to swing a horizontal butt stroke at your head.

Deflect the rifle butt up with a forearm, changing the plane or orientation of the circle.

Deflect the rising rifle butt...

Inward and upward.

Quickly step in and execute an uppercut into his chin.

Lunging butt stroke defense

1

The attacker prepares to plunge the butt of his rifle into your face.

2

Deflect the butt upward with your forearm.

3

Grab the rifle barrel as it rises to meet you and the stock as it continues upward and backward.

4

Pull away the barrel and stock, destroying his balance.

5

As he stumbles forward, spin around and watch him pass.

6

Immediately counter with a thrust to his back.

You see, it *is* possible to deal with the rifle and bayonet.

CHAPTER 11

Unarmed Defenses Against Chokes

Because chokes attack two major body systems, breathing and blood flow to the brain, many people don't know how to defend against them. If you learn a few rules and remember to apply the Universal Force Dynamics principles and factors, chokes should not pose that serious a threat.

Rear choke defense

The most important rule to remember is to quickly tuck your chin and point it into your opponent's inside bent elbow.

The second rule is to be as aggressive as possible. As soon as the attacker starts to apply the choke, jam your thumb into the nerve center of his elbow. Begin to throw your hips back and to the side. This is known as "going out the back door."

Scoot out the back door, but keep control of his arm.

Apply a hammer lock...

To gain time to get full control of your opponent.

Rear elbow strike

Front bar choke defenses

As you are grabbed...

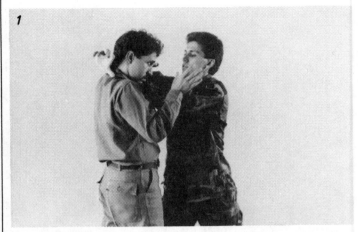

As your attacker applies the choke, tuck your chin to protect your throat.

Execute a rear elbow strike into his ribs or solar plexus to loosen his choke.

Then thumb gouge his eyes.

Front hand choke — Body weight release

As your attacker begins to choke you with his hands...

Raise your hand and pivot in while...

Stepping forward. Insert your arm between his arms and...

Drive your hand all the way to the ground. Your body weight will break his grip.

As soon as your hand reaches the ground, execute an elbow strike upward into his groin, stomach, or chin.

Neck-breaker release

As your attacker attempts to choke, grab the front of his jacket and...

Execute a palm strike to his chin while you pull him forward. If you do this quickly, you will break his neck.

Escape from a choke on the ground

Grab one of your attacker's elbows with both hands and...

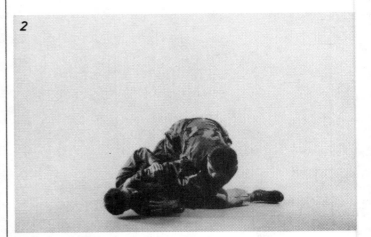

Pull him violently across your body.

Side headlock release

1

When you're grabbed in a side headlock...

2

Reach up to claw his face while you...

3

Push the face backward and lift his nearby leg to dump him on his head.

Front headlock release

1

When an attacker puts on a front choking headlock on you...

2

Uppercut a fist into his groin.

Garrot defense

As the garrot drops over your head, raise your hand so that it is...

Inside the encircling threat.

Extend your other hand forward and...

Counter with an elbow strike to the rear.

CHAPTER 12

Unarmed Defenses Against Kicks

Blocking a kick is based upon the same principle as blocking a strike. The only difference is that kicks are more powerful and can strike lower targets. This makes them more dangerous than strikes.

You can avoid them by moving back...

To the side...

Or to the front and side.

Many of the following defenses begin by first avoiding the kick. These are primarily hapkido defenses. They seek to simultaneously disrupt and set up a counterattack.

Front kick deflection

From the on-guard position...

Step slightly outside...

And deflect the kick inward so that it passes by.

Front kick X-block

Bend down to meet the kick...

With crossed wrists (the x). Don't try to block the kick. Catch it instead and...

Lift the foot to lead him off balance. Then counterfront kick to his groin.

Knee kick jam

As the attacker attempts to knee you in the groin...

Deflect it outside with your own knee, turning his force.

Side kick scoop

From the on-guard position...

Scoop the back of the attacker's heel.

This will turn him around to a vulnerable position. Be sure to return your hand to a high-line guard position.

Side kick deflection

1

As the kick comes in, deflect it with a forearm.

2

This will swing him around and place you in an advantageous position.

Rising block

1

As the kick comes out...

2

Pick it up with your rising forearm. Lean back and counter with a side kick of your own into his groin or inner thigh.

Low kick unweighting

When the attacker executes a low kick into your knee...

Move your weight to your rear leg and raise your targeted leg. This nullifies the more dangerous effects of the low kick.

Low kick avoid

As the attacker kicks...

Move back out of the way.

High roundhouse jam

When an attacker attempts a high roundhouse kick to your face...

Jam it with your forearm.

Low roundhouse scoop

Catch the roundhouse kick in a scoop and...

Shinbone kick his knee to break it.

96

Side kick outside-catch/knee break

Step outside to catch the leg.

Grab his shoulder and swing your leg through and then back into his locked knee.

This will throw him on his face while it breaks his knee.

Side kick inside catch/knee break

Step in to catch the leg.

Step in front of his locked knee and...

Throw him to his face while breaking his knee.

Side kick catch and throw

Step outside to catch the leg.

Grab the foot as shown and...

Twist it to force the attacker to rotate horizontally in the air. (If your opponent resists this, try lowering his foot a little while you twist).

As soon as he lands on his back, stomp the inside of his knee while you wrench his other leg out to tear his groin tendons.

Step over the held leg and drive down your body weight to dislocate his knee and hip joints.

Inside crescent jam

As the attacker attempts to bring a crescent kick to the inside, jam it with your forearm.

Outside crescent counter

Duck under and...

Uppercut into his groin.

CHAPTER 13

Unarmed Defenses Against Throws

After you have mastered the throws in Chapter 5, you should learn how to defend yourself against all throws. The secret to successful throwing defenses is to destroy your opponent's balance before he destroys yours. The following techniques don't include every option; however, they will give you a feel for how the theory is applied. For specific counters, read a good book on judo techniques.

Shoulder throw defense

As your opponent pulls you in and pivots...

Apply a palm strike to his kidney to disrupt his throw.

Pull him backward until he...

Falls and follow up with a strike.

Hip throw defense

As your opponent pulls you in and starts to step through...

Quickly step through the opening between your bodies, placing your hip behind his hip.

Reverse hip roll him over onto his head.

Back trip defense

As your opponent begins his trip...

Violently lunge forward breaking his balance...

And push him to the ground.

CHAPTER 14

Unarmed Defenses Against Holds and Grabs

The following escapes are taken from Combatives, hapkido and wrestling. Although there are hundreds of techniques, these are the simplest and surest.

Rear Bear Hug Escapes

Groin attack

When your attacker grabs you in a bear hug from the rear, immediately thrust your hips forward.

Violently thrust your hips back into his groin while throwing your arms forward to loosen his grip.

Move your hips to the side, make a fist, and sight in on your target. Execute a backfist to his groin.

Wrist lock

1

If the attacker clasps his own wrist to make his bear hug more powerful...

2

Grab his arm just above his grip to stabilize his arm. At the same time, press your palm against the back of his hand, forcing his wrist into a painfully locked position.

3

Keep his wrist in a lock.

4

Pivot out of the bear hug.

5

Front kick into his face.

Foot stomp

As you are hugged, raise one foot...

And stomp your heel onto his instep, breaking the small bones on the top of his foot.

Head butt

You can also use a head butt to the rear into your opponent's face to loosen his grip.

Front bear hug escapes

Ear drum shatter

1

If you are grabbed in a front bear hug under your arms, immediately swing your arms back and cup your hands.

2

Slap your cupped hands over his ear holes. This will simultaneously shatter his ear drums and disturb the balancing mechanism in his inner ear.

Neck break

As you are hugged, place a palm under his chin and push it around while you pull down on his head with your other hand. If done quickly and forcefully, it will break his neck.

Front bar arm choke

When you are hugged, choke him with a bar arm. Even if your attacker pulls you down to the ground, he is at a disadvantage as long as you maintain the choke.

Groin strike

1

If you are hugged over your arms so that they are tied up, make your hands into fists with your thumbs extended.

2

Slam both thumbs forward into his groin or pubic bone region.

Head butt

You can use a head butt forward with your forehead into his face to obtain a release.

Defenses against held wrists

Many throws, locks, and come-alongs begin with a wrist grab. Defenses against these situations are considered so important in hapkido that 35 escapes must be mastered to progress from beginner (white belt) to the next stage (blue belt). Another 20 must be mastered for the next stage of red belt (which is just below first-degree black belt). We will address only a few here. You will also find extensive techniques in the arts of hwarang do, jujitsu, and chin na, the northern Chinese grappling art.

The first step in escaping a wrist grab is to open your hand as wide as possible.

Live hand

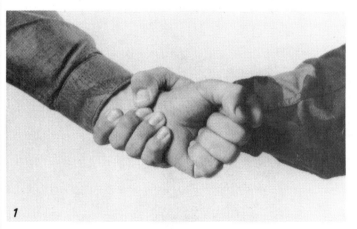

1

Here we see a hand around a wrist. The defender has closed his fist.

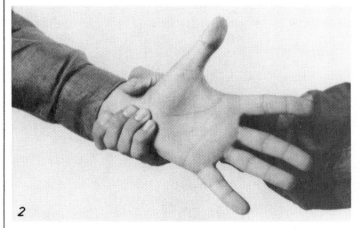

2

Now we see the defender's hand open wide in what hap-kidoists call a "live hand." Notice that the opening of the hand has caused the defender's wrist to greatly expand and the attacker's grip to loosen.

Old faithful escape

As your wrist is grabbed, open your hand into the "live hand" position and...

Rotate your held hand to the outside so that his wrist is placed in the "V" formed by your thumb and first finger. At the same time, place the other side of his hand into the "V" of your free hand.

Having stabilized your opponent, pivot in and pull his arm through until it is under your armpit.

Continue your turn, rotating your armpit down and levering his arm up. This will break his elbow and force him to the floor.

Hammerfist escape

As your wrist is grabbed, strike the nerve point in his forearm muscle...

With a hammerfist. This will loosen his grip.

Immediately wind up and...

Strike your opponent's face with a hammerfist to the cheek bone. It should take less than a second to complete both strikes.

Cross-wrist lock

1

If your opponent reaches across to grab your wrist with his opposite hand...

2

Rotate your wrist around to the outside of his arm and clamp your fingers onto it. At the same time, clasp your free hand onto the top of his holding hand so he cannot withdraw it. Raise the clamped arm up...

3

Step forward, and...

4

Rotate your hand down and forward. This will break his wrist and tear out several arm tendons if done quickly. If done slower, it will place him in excruciating pain and will make him very controllable.

110

Escaping the full nelson

As your opponent clamps on a full-nelson hold...

Reach up to either side and grab a finger (preferably the ring finger).

Lever the finger back and pivot to the outside.

Step forward into the fingerlock position.

Pull-aways

After expanding your hand, simply pull or push against your opponent's thumb...

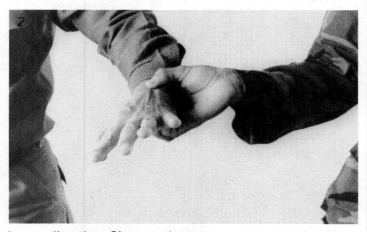

In any direction. Since we know we can control the situation, we may want to punish our opponent as we pull away.

CHAPTER 15

Fighting from the Ground

You may find yourself having to fight from the ground against a standing opponent. Don't give up; you actually can be very deadly from this position. Be calm and aggressive!

Defending to the front

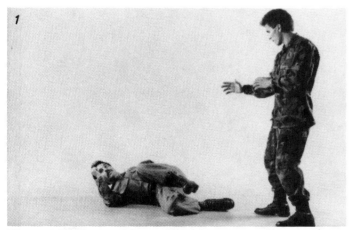

First, get on your side and hip. Keep your bottom leg on the ground for stability and raise the other to give it maneuverability. Anchor your upper body with your hands and raise your head a little so you can see what's going on.

As your opponent moves in, hook your bottom foot behind his heel and...

Stomp his knee to break it.

Defending to the side

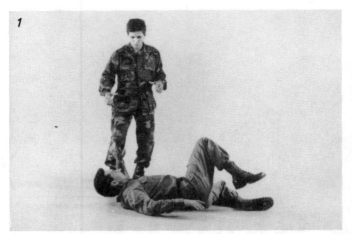

As your opponent approaches from the side, chamber your upper knee back and...

Let fly a pointed toe kick into his groin.

Defending against a stomp

As your attacker raises his foot, quickly raise your hands and...

Catch his foot before it gains too much momentum.

Twist his foot sharply and dump him on the ground.

Defending against an arm bar choke from a body straddle

1

Since the arm bar choke is very painful and dangerous . . .

2

Quickly go for the thumb gouge . . .

3

And he will release his grip.

Attacking from the side

1

If your opponent tries to groin kick you as you come in from the side...

2

Quickly jam his leg with your forearm before the kick builds too much momentum.

Attacking a grounded person from the front

As your grounded opponent begins a kick...

Scoop block his heel as you would a side kick when you are both standing.

Throw his leg over out of the way and...

Immediately dive onto his back and strike him or choke him.

Attacking the head

If your opponent looks too alert, don't try a stomp that can be easily caught.

Simply placekick his head out of the stadium.

CHAPTER 16

Knife Fighting

There are a multitude of ways to fight with a knife. Some, like Filipino balisong knife fighting, are highly complex and very fast and flashy. Others are more conservative. While some street forms may appear to be macho, they are almost downright foolish. The style used in this chapter is conservative, tried and proven, and easily learned.

A good fighting knife should be small enough to allow your wrist to move easily and large enough to allow for penetration into major internal organs. The blade should be at least four inches and no more than 12 inches long (any longer than that and you're using a short sword, not a knife). The knife should be made of a strong steel that is not too brittle (and, therefore, likely to break). The guard should be of a softer metal such as brass to trap an incoming edge. The balance of the knife should be just behind the guard. There are many excellent custom-made fighting knives;

however, they are generally expensive. Some of the best factory-made fighting knives are from Portland, Ore., at Gerber Knife Company. However, don't use them as a utility knife. They are designed solely for killing people, not hacking out paths through the underbrush. The old Marine K-Bar knife is a good all-around weapon but is less effective for fighting because of the heaviness of its blade (which is what makes it so good for utility work).

The Fairborn-Sykes, famous World War II British commando knife, is best used as a stabbing dagger because of its narrow blade and small diameter grip. In other words, there is no such thing as a "perfect" knife for all jobs. Therefore, many soldiers carry two knives: one for camp and bush work and another for fighting. If you find a knife that will serve well in either capacity, be grateful and treat it as a treasure.

Grips

The secret to superior knife fighting is wrist flexibility, mobility and strength. The wrist provides the final cutting movement, angle and pressure as the knife passes into the flesh. For this reason, the grip of the knife is critical to the fighter's success.

The classic ice-pick grip is limited in its range of motion. Some martial artists may use a modified ice-pick grip that lays the back of the blade under the forearm in an attempt to hide or disguise the direction of the blade. This too is limited because it requires gross movements of the arm to create significant changes in blade angles. The hammergrip is the most limited in movement. It also requires gross arm movements for blade angle adjustments.

The saber grip is among the best for wrist mobility and strength. It is surpassed only by the...

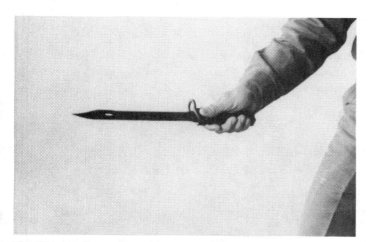

Modified saber grip, which rotates the knife onto its side. This orientation is also the best for thrusting into the rib area.

Stances

The way you hold your body is just as important as how you hold your knife. A good stance should allow both security and mobility.

Although very theatrical in appearance, this stance brings the knife too far forward. It is vulnerable to a snapping front kick and its movements are there for all the world to see.

Although the knife is now further back, the groin and body are too open to attacks from blade or foot.

This is an ideal stance because the knife is back out of the way and yet it may strike out quickly. The free hand is also in a better position to block or screen the opponent's view of your knife.

119

Targets

There are two classes of targets: secondary and primary. Secondary targets are generally safer and easier to attack. They generally incapacitate. Primary targets are potentially fatal and, therefore, are more difficult to hit. A good rule is to attack the secondary targets first to slow or disarm your opponent. Then, go for the primary targets when they can no longer be effectively protected.

Secondary targets

Finger cut.

Outside wrist or hand tendon cut.

Inner wrist tendon/artery cut.

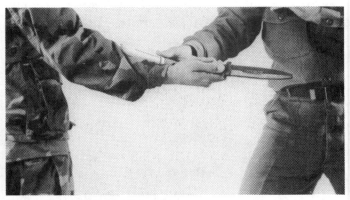

Forearm tendon/nerve cut.

Forehead cut (blood flows into eyes, temporarily blinding the opponent).

Hamstringing behind the knee or ankle.

Primary targets

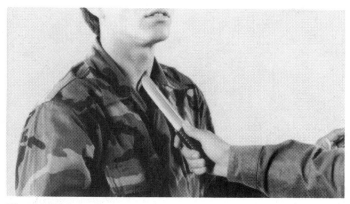

Throat stab.

Inner thigh (femoral artery).

Groin stab.

Correct method of slipping in between or through the ribs (see the modified saber grip).

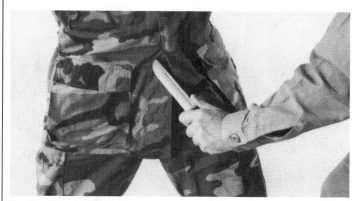

Body thrust (note the upward angle).

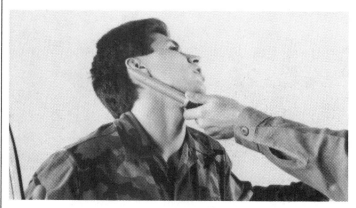

Throat slash.

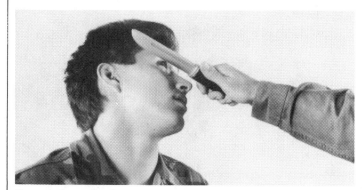

Eye stab or slash.

Blocks

The most effective blocks are those made by a blade against the flesh. Kicks can also be used as a counter while the block is being executed.

A back slash begins and...

Is blocked by a cut to the outer wrist.

Block thrust by cutting the wrist.

A thrust is blocked while a knee is taken out with a kick.

Offensive combinations

An inner wrist cut is made...

Followed by a...

Body thrust.

A high thrust is attacked...

Followed by a throat slice.

Tie-ups

If you tie-up with your opponent, attempt to cut a secondary target at the same time.

Low tie-up and...

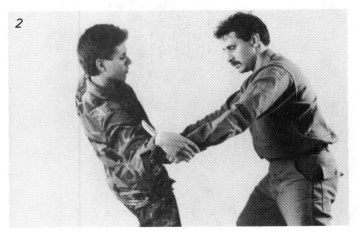

Cut.

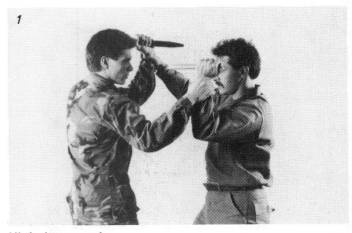

High tie-up and...

Cut.

Shields

You can protect your arm by wrapping your shirt or jacket around it. This may temporarily catch an opponent's blade and screen your own blade from view. Items such as belts may also be used.

Practice

For safety reasons, do not practice knife fighting with real blades. Use wooden knives or sawed-off broom handles to get a feel for distance and balance. The wooden replica also lends a degree of realism when your training partner connects. Rubber replicas do not create a sense of danger.

CHAPTER 17

Sentry Neutralization

The imperatives for taking out a sentry are silence and speed through the use of your bare hands, knife, or a garrot. Whatever you use, don't allow your enemy to sound the alarm.

Garrot

Drop the garrot...

Over the sentry's head and cross its ends.

Pivot and hang him over your shoulder. In that way, you are letting his body weight do the work for you instead of having to muscle your way against his neck muscles with your arms.

Knife techniques

As you make your approach, clamp you hand over both the nostrils and mouth of the sentry to cut off any sound.

Plunge your knife into his kidney. This is a high shock-producing injury which causes its victim to inhale sharply (which is cut off by your hand).

Withdraw the knife and plunge it straight into the side of his neck and...

Force it forward to cut the neck's major arteries and windpipe. This will cause unconsciousness and death in seconds while maintaining silence. It is also much neater than cutting the throat from ear to ear around the front which sprays blood over a wide area and may allow noise to escape the windpipe. With the preferred method, the windpipe fills with blood, internally silencing the sound of air escaping.

Another swift method is to plunge the knife straight down into the subclavian artery area and move it back and forth. Blood pressure drops precipitiously.

Neck-breaker

Cover his mouth and nose and punch him powerfully in the kidney.

Slip your hand down and across his throat while pulling back.

Pull your choke tight, throw your feet back, and drop him to the ground to break his neck. (Be extremely careful when practicing this).

CHAPTER 18

Expedient Weapons

On the battlefield, it's OK to use anything as a weapon in self-defense. Firing a rock at an attacker's head is likely to slow him. So will dirt or sand thrown in his eyes. Flicking a lit cigarette into his face and following it up with a blow is also a great distractor. An aerosol can and a cigarette lighter or flaming stick make excellent flamethrowers. Several agents in World War II used sharpened pencils against their guards' eyes, jugular veins, or ear holes to successfully escape.

If your foe has the only weapon, prepare to pick up anything and start swinging. If you read the citations for bravery of Congressional Medal of Honor winners, you will get a graphic picture of what close-quarters combat must be like. The following two citations beautifully illustrate this point. They were paraphrased from incidents recorded in *The Congressional Medal of Honor: The Names, The Deeds.* Sharp & Dunnigan Publications, Forest Ranch, CA 1984.

First Lieutenant (then Master Sergeant) Benjamin F. Wilson, U.S. Army, near Hwa Chon Myon, Korea, on June 5, 1951, charged an enemy counterattack single-handedly, killing seven and wounding two, causing their attack to fail. Later, he again charged the enemy, killing three enemy soldiers with his rifle before it was wrestled from his hands. He then killed four more with his entrenching tool (small shovel). For this action, he was awarded the Congressional Medal of Honor.

Sergeant Harold O. Messerschmidt, U.S. Army, near Radden, France, on September 17, 1944, was knocked to the ground by a burst from an enemy automatic weapon. He ignored his severe wounds, fired his submachine gun at the enemy that was now upon his position and killed five and wounded many others before his ammunition was spent. Although surrounded by the enemy, and all his squad now casualties, he elected to fight alone, using his empty submachine gun as a bludgeon against his assailants. Spotting one of the enemy about to kill a wounded comrade, he felled the attacker with a blow from his weapon. He also received the Medal of Honor for his actions.

Can lid shuriken

Although "C"-rations are being phased out, there are still plenty of can lids available in garrison. They make excellent expedient throwing stars or shuriken. Store a couple in your battle-dress uniform breast pockets. They won't kill, but they will distract an oncoming enemy. Like the ninja throwing star, they are not meant to kill. However, imagine the effect a spinning sharp metal disk can have on an eye (blinding) or forehead (cause blood to flow into the eyes).

A can lid can either be backhanded or overhanded. Use a lot of wrist action. They'll fly true for 10-15 feet, giving you time to close with the enemy or dodge and hide.

Clubs

From Chapter 8: Unarmed Defenses Against Club Attacks, we learn that clubs can be neutralized, especially if they're big and long. A more effective club is the billy club or shortened night stick. The secret to effective club use is in the wrist action. Strikes should be made with short, snappy motions that are hard to track visually by the enemy.

Overhand strike

The club is held loosely in your hand, primarily by the little and ring fingers. Note that the business end of the club is held away from its target.

The wrist and little fingers snap the club forward and down onto the wristbone of the attacker.

Backhand strike

Again the club begins pointed away.

It remains so until the last second when it...

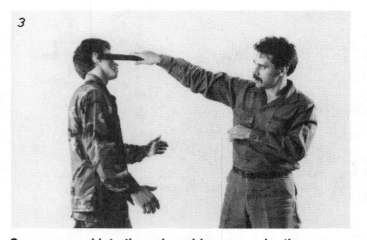

Snaps around into the vulnerable area under the ear.

Thrust

The club can be thrust into...

An opponent's solar plexus.

Butt stroke

The butt end of the club can be...

Hammered down into nerve or muscle vital points.

For more information on the proper use of a club, see the chapter on the Short Fighting Stick in the author's book, *Hapkido: The Integrated Fighting Art.* Unique Publications.

Bandanna Garrot

One of the easiest ways to make an expedient garrot is to roll up and fold the bandanna into a triangle. Roll it up into a tight tube.

Wrap it around the first two fingers of each hand. It is now ready to be dropped over a sentry's head.

Another expedient garrot is the use of two sticks for handles and a guitar or piano string for the actual garrot. Survival wire saws with a toothed wire and two metal ring handles are the best makeshift garrots because they lock together once tension is applied.

Konga

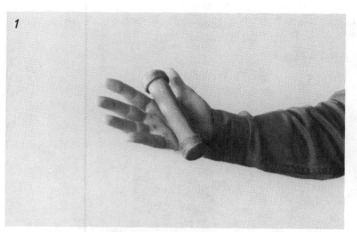

The Konga is a short piece of hardwood dowel rod that has been turned down on a lathe to form two dumbbell-like ends.

It is held in your fist and can be used to...

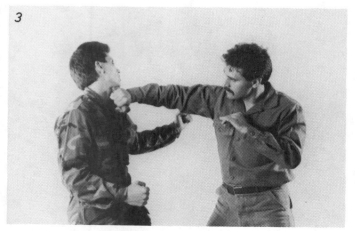

Strike with a hammerfist...

Strike with a fist (supporting the hand like a roll of quarters)...

Or strike with an upstroke. It is used against joints, nerve, and muscle vital points, and as a hard-blocking instrument.

SECTION II
Installing Martial Arts Into Unit Training

CHAPTER 19

Training Female Soldiers

The U.S. military has been known to lead the rest of our society in social reform. The women in our service have attained a number of equal rights: equal pay, equal education, and an equal chance to die for their country. The Army does not allow female soldiers into combat units that must serve on the front lines; however, as we discussed in the introduction, females in the rear areas are quite likely to come under enemy fire and personal attack. Unfortunately, the Army doesn't teach its ladies in the rank and file how to defend themselves. At least they are not being discriminated against; the Army doesn't teach its male soldiers to defend themselves either.

For this reason, the techniques in this book have been purposely designed for easy execution by both male and female soldiers. Although male models were used, every one of the movements demonstrated are sexless in terms of do-ability. There is one difference, however, that cannot be rectified by a book. The reason why many ladies can't fight is because they've never been culturally programmed as warriors. Old "dad" may take his little boy aside to teach him some of the manly arts and responses when he comes home from the playground with a bloody nose, but "little girls don't fight!" Not only that, "boys shouldn't hit girls." Because of these cultural quirks, most girls never learn how to make a fist, properly throw a punch, or fight their way out of trouble (see Chapter 22 — Mental Conditioning with the Martial Arts).

If you are responsible for a military unit training program, take this social conditioning into consideration. Initially segregate your training program at first so your females get a better handle on the basics without having to be embarrassed by their male counterparts. Once they have physically mastered what many of the men already know, they will still need some mental toughening. Use role models and myths from other battles and cultures to illustrate that women are capable of defending themselves and others. They must understand the better they are at personal combat, the more respect and trust their male counterparts will have for them. This *must* take place if you are going to have unit cohesiveness.

Once your ladies have toughened up, bring them gradually into a mixed-sex training environment. If you find that a very few are already tough cookies, use them as role models for others. Consider making them assistant instructors (AIs).

With the proper training and conditioning, women can become awesome fighters. One incident from the early 1970s comes to mind. The U.S. Army was just beginning a rapid increase of minority and female soldier recruiting to make up for significant post-Vietnam-draft personnel shortages. Although South Korea was one country where few female soldiers had ever served, our unit suddenly got word that at least 50 females were en route for assignment. There was mixed reaction to this news. Strangely enough, the most negative reaction was from other females, specifically Korean prostitutes who plied their trade in the village just off post. The young ladies of the night viewed the presence of female troops as unfair competition. Unbeknownst to our soldiers, battle lines were drawn and a test confrontation was planned. The first night our new girls were in-country, some of the guys invited them out for a few drinks at a local bar our unit frequented. Three of the girls agreed to go with about 20 of the guys. As soon as everyone sat down, the Korean girls started talking among themselves. Three of these locals selected a likely looking victim. Their purpose was to see just what American girls were made of. Unfortunately, they happened to choose a girl nicknamed "Fred". Although Fred looked quite harmless, she had been raised in a rough, Appalachian coal-mining town. In her neighborhood the only way a girl kept her virginity past the age of 12 was to be fleet of foot and be able to fight like a wildcat.

The three Koreans began calling her names. When she didn't react, one made the mistake of grabbing Fred by the hair and pulling her from her chair. A major cat fight ensued. The three locals were trying to jump her, but Fred concentrated on their leader, the one who instigated the incident. It ended with Fred having her hands around the leader's neck, and methodically banging the girl's head into the wall. The remaining Korean women tried to pull Fred off, but she simply ignored them. Finally, when Fred thought the leader had had enough, she stopped banging her head and told her in no uncertain terms that she should think twice before jumping another American girl. The outcome was far-reaching. Not only were the American girls left alone, but some of the Korean girls became friends with Fred. After all, they surely didn't want her as an enemy. They also passed the word not to mess with the American newcomers. We often wondered what would have happened if the Korean girls had picked on an easy target instead of Fred. Or, what would have happened if the guys had jumped in too soon? Perhaps Fred's fighting ability saved the American/Korean community from a damaging breakdown in relations. Subsequently, the transition for our female troops was much easier after Fred took control.

CHAPTER 20

The Threat

When the military writes doctrine for a new concept or a requirement document for a new weapons system, a major concern is the specific enemy threat. If our soldiers experienced hand-to-hand combat on the battlefield, what types of techniques are they likely to encounter? What kind of combative training will the enemy soldier have had? Who conducted the enemy's training? What mastery level have their soldiers attained and how current is their training? What role does fighting play in their cultural background?

This chapter will answer some of these questions about our most likely foes, the Communist Bloc countries and Middle East terrorists. The challenge was to get the information through unclassified security-level channels. For that reason, all sources of information are available in periodicals or non-governmental interviews with eyewitnesses.

A conversation a few years ago with a Warsaw-Pact nation defector who had been a military officer revealed that for three years of officer school, he had received an average of five-to-eight hours of hand-to-hand training per week. He said all officer trainees received the same amount of training. When he was told our Army had discontinued their Combatives program in the early 1970s, he was flabbergasted.

"How can you possibly keep your troops in line?" he said. This says a lot about Communist leadership techniques. He also said they consider hand-to-hand fighting to be essential soldier and officer battle skills. Let's look at some specific training programs and cultural traditions of the major threat countries and their role in military training.

The Soviet Union

The Russians are deadly serious about the amount and realism of their hand-to-hand training. In an April, 1986, *Reader's Digest* article, *Spetsnaz: The Soviets' Sinister Strike Force*, by Dale Van Atta, the author quotes the famous Soviet defector/author Viktor Suvorov. The Spetsnaz is the Soviet equivalent to our Special Forces except that it doesn't perceive training as a primary mission; it orients on rear area disruption and the assassination of key leaders. He wrote, "Sheer brutality marks the Spetsnaz methods. One of their main training centers at Zheltyye Vody in the Ukraine — is close to concentration camps. According to Suvorov, gulag inmates are used in hand-to-hand combat training, allowing Spetsnaz troops to punch, gouge, kick and maim at will. It's much more realistic than sticking a knife in a sack of sand."

For many years, the primary martial art in the Soviet Union was sambo, a combination of judo (brought over by the Japanese before the turn of the century) and Mongolian wrestling. Their military used sambo training (often conducted on bare ground or floors without mats) for battle-hardening drills and fighting skills.

Now their military is much more sophisticated. The following excerpts are from an article written by Colonel V. Safonov in the Soviet military journal, *Voyennyy Vestnik*, No. 7, 1984, pp. 36-39. Titled, "For Victory in Hand-to-Hand Combat," the article describes training in a typical Soviet airborne assault unit (the kind most likely to be found in our rear areas).

Learning the proper techniques is the key to beating a stronger opponent, the article stresses. You will find they have been studying for several years the types of subjects advocated for our own troops.

Colonel Safonov stated, "During classes in hand-to-hand combat against the enemy, airborne assault troops develop fighting skills, boldness, resolve, initiative, resourcefulness, self-confidence, composure and self-control. Special 16-count moves with and without weapons are included in the course content along with preparatory exercises, self-defense techniques, leg and arm blows and defenses against them, strangulation techniques, and throws. Various methods of tying up the enemy are practiced using improvised means, escaping from an escort under various situations, and other techniques and actions. Classes are also held in the gymnasiums; in classrooms with special equipment, trainers, and auxiliary apparatus; and under field conditions on a level, grassy area. Bayonet thrusts, blows with a knife, shovel, and rifle butt, and throwing a knife, shovel, metal plate, and other piercing objects are practiced on training dummies, mannequins, and targets. At the end of each class there is a comprehensive training session on a rotation method or in the form of sparring where an individual works against one, two, or three persons using previously studied techniques."

The instructors are commissioned officers and warrants, many of whom hold Masters of Sport degrees. After they have warmed up the soldiers with flexibility and speed/strength/endurance exercises, they conduct round-robin training at five or six stations. A typical training session's organization appears below:

First training station

Fighting stances, moves and turns, attacking arms and leg thrusts, and defenses or blocks against arm and leg thrusts.

Second training station

Methods of throwing a knife or bayonet, a small sapper shovel, and other piercing objects from various positions.

Third training station

Possible training situations in hand-to-hand combat against several enemies armed with a variety of weapons. The trainees determine the type of defense and attack techniques to be applied and orient themselves spatially on the spot and in a combat situation.

Fourth training station

Methods of tying up an enemy using a trouser belt, ropes, or lines, an airborne backpack, and a stick.

Fifth training station

Free sparring with both one-on-one and multiple opponent situations. Colonel Safonov stated, "It must be noted that during near-real sparring, the airborne assault troops develop a unique tactic for conducting hand-to-hand fighting, a sense of distance, and necessary psychological qualities. The effectiveness of thrusts, blocks, and slaps also is checked out in a specific situation. Blows are delivered quickly at about one-third the normal force. Full contact is permitted in protective suits. The privates and NCOs were extremely composed and attentive in the practice contests, especially the group contests. They constantly watched their opponents' actions and the movement of their hands, feet, and torso. All the while they maintained the optimum distance and tried to anticipate the opponent's blow. The sparring was intense. On closing, the soldiers employed throws and blows with the elbows, knees and head. In every convenient situation they attacked boldly and delivered blows with concentration, accuracy, speed and at full strength. They did not tighten their muscles, they kept their bodies relaxed and were ready to react instantaneously to the opponent's actions, and they maneuvered constantly."

North Korea

Like their southern neighbors, the North Koreans have a strong cultural background in the martial arts tae kwon do and hapkido, which are exclusively South Korean arts developed since 1945. Taekyung is similar to some of the northern Chinese kung-fu styles. It has circular movements, many low kicks, and some eagle claw ripping and gouging techniques. Soldiers are taught these techniques along with field expedient weapons. They study several kata (memorized movement/technique combinations) using the entrenching shovel as a weapon. Their special operation troops have been known to conduct extensive hand-conditioning and brick-breaking exercises. And, the North Koreans play a major role in training the world's revolutionary terrorist organizations.

China

The government of the People's Republic of China fully supports the maintenance of its martial arts heritage. Along with a government-sponsored wu shu (martial art) demonstration team, China is proposing the inclusion of some of its styles in the tae kwon do demonstration fighting events at the 1988 Olympics in Seoul, Korea. Although the martial arts permeate society, not much is known about the specifics of its military's hand-to-hand training programs. It is unclear whether teachers use a traditional style or if they favor an amalgamation of several.

Middle East terrorists

The North Koreans have been the primary training advisers to various Middle East terrorist organizations for over 15 years. Terrorists continually travel to North Korea to train in special camps. North Korean advisers have traveled to terrorist training camps in Lebanon, Libya and Syria, as well as other hotbeds of terrorist activity. Interestingly, the North Koreans are teaching classes on thanatology or death acceptance to terrorists being considered for suicide missions.

The fighting techniques being taught are mainly ripping and gouging techniques aimed at the eyes, ears and nose. Standard street-fighting movements are also being taught.

The fighting tradition throughout the Middle East is wrestling. Almost every village has a local champion. Another tradition is the use of bladed weapons.

Iran

According to the teen-aged son of a former colonel in the Shah's Army, hand-to-hand fighting is being taught at the middle school level. The son had been trained in street fighting as part of his rudimentary revolutionary military training. He stated his teachers were a trainer who studied at the Kodokan Judo University in Tokyo, and a kung-fu stylist who mastered "toa" in Hong Kong. This style may have been a Farsi adulturation of the Chinese word "tao" (the equivalent of the Japanese term "do" or "the way").

Wrestling and weightlifting are very strong traditions in Iran. Male machismo is a way of life. Expect strong grappling techniques from Iranian soldiers.

Cuba

As Soviet surrogate forces, the Cubans receive the same training as Russian troops. They also are strong in the areas of boxing and bladed weapons. Many soldiers have had extensive experience with sugar-cane knives.

CHAPTER 21

Physical Conditioning with the Martial Arts

The Training Schedule Challenge

Until now we have talked mostly about the need to teach a good personal combat system that features effective techniques. However, we must find time to teach the skills while vying with many other training subjects and bureaucratic distractions. Fortunately, there is time available for martial art workouts on most unit training schedules. The Army's Physical Fitness Center at the Soldiers Support Center, Fort Ben Harrison, Indianapolis, Ind., has produced an excellent pamphlet (DA PAM 350-15) called "*The Commander's Handbook on Physical Fitness.*" This pamphlet recommends that a typical unit schedule might consist of one hour of physical conditioning per day, five days per week. It stresses the importance of variety and regularity. The schedule for Mondays, Wednesdays and Fridays includes stretching, a long run, and a cool-down period, followed by physical activities such as sit-ups, push-ups and chin-ups. On Tuesdays and Thursdays, it recommends activities such as obstacle courses, unit sports and road marches. Martial art training could easily be incorporated as supplementary programs into the Tuesday/Thursday session. It could even replace — on a temporary basis — the primary activities on Mondays, Wednesdays, and Fridays when added emphasis is needed to ready the unit for combat-level proficiency.

Expected outcomes

If we use the martial arts as a physical conditioning activity, we should understand how participants' bodies will be enhanced. The following outcomes can be expected:

Flexibility

The martial arts emphasize body and limb flexibility to gain speed, power, agility, full range of joint movement, and to lessen the likelihood of training and combat injuries. Although the combat techniques taught here don't demand the degree of flexibility required in most arts, they will be more effective if you are flexible.

Strength/endurance

Both the combat movements and the recommended exercises will increase your strength and endurance in muscle groups necessary for effective combat. In other words, the physical activity is combat specific, and every effort has a logical purpose.

Agility/reactions

Exploding into movement suddenly and effectively is endemic to personal combat. Increased reaction development aids agility simply through practice and repetition. If the range of movement becomes "programmed" into your reactions, grace and ease also will be learned.

Balance

Effective combat requires total self-control, and it all begins with balance. It's difficult to be effective with a blow or counter if you're off balance. A common martial arts expression, "being grounded," means being physically in touch with the earth and with your stance and movement at all times.

Capability to close with and kill the enemy

The main difference between physical condition exercises and the martial arts is that exercise will get you fit while martial arts will get you fit as it teaches you to survive.

The Fort Lewis experiments

It is not enough to talk about the martial arts effect on enhancing physical abilities. Sooner or later, the claims must be proven. And so the Army's chief of staff declared 1982 the year of physical fitness in the Army. He challenged all commanders to raise their commands' level of fitness. The High Technology Test Bed was tasked by the commanding general of the 9th Infantry Division at Fort Lewis, Wash., to evaluate several new exercise regimens and compare them to the standard Army conditioning drills. Four regimens were selected for evaluation:

1. *The standard army physical fitness system*, based upon calisthenics and a two-mile run.

2. *Manual resistance training*, developed at The Pennsylvania State University by Dr. Dan Riley, who is now the Washington Redskins' strength coach. This was based on two soldiers working together. One provided the resistance and the other exercised.

3. *Close-quarters combat combatives*, based upon

Professor Ray Wood's West Point Military Academy martial arts program. It was comprised of exercises and techniques taken from Combatives, hapkido, judo and karate.

4. *Combat obstacle course, combat cross-country run*, based on the running of an obstacle course for time and a three-mile run in combat boots.

Evaluation concept

A statistically significant population of test subjects were drawn from three types of battalions: a combat infantry battalion, a combat engineer battalion, and a logistics/medical support battalion (the latter having an abundance of female soldiers). In each battalion, four companies were involved. One company was assigned to each alternative. There were at least 225 test subjects in each of the four regimens. Each group trained in its respective regimen for ten weeks. Pre and post-training physical tests recorded changes in the participants' physical and emotional status over the ten weeks.

Physical tests

Immediately before the ten-weeks training period, the pretraining baseline test was administered to all participants. This consisted of:

1. The number of push-ups executed in two minutes (tricep strength).

2. The number of sit-ups executed in two minutes (abdominal and upper thigh strength).

3. The number of pull-ups executed in two minutes (bicep strength).

4. The reach forward while seated with straight legs to the front and stretching one's arms forward as far as possible (lower back flexibility).

5. A two-mile run for time in running shoes instead of combat boots.

After the ten-week period, the same test was administered and performance changes were noted. Here are the results:

Mean Group Performance Changes

Condition	Pull-up	Push-up	Sit-up	Run	Reach
Std PT	+.7	+1.6	-.2	+32.2	-3.4
Man Resist	No Change	+5.7	+2.5	+4.3	+2.0
CQC/Cbt	+1.0	+4.6	+6.9	-65.0	+3.0
Cbt Obstl Crs	-1.1	+6.8	+2.9	-35.1	+2.6

As shown, the Close-Quarters Combat/Combatives (Martial Arts) regimen had the best scores in four of the five events. In all, the martial arts are as good if not better than most conditioning regimens. Interestingly the standard Army PT regimen showed the worst performance in four of the five events.

The Dallas Cowboys Experience

Dr. Bob Ward, conditioning coach of the Dallas Cowboys of the National Football League, has been using martial art exercises for over eight years to improve player skills. Ward, a long-time student of Dan Inosanto, has used drills from jeet kune do, wing chun and Thai boxing to improve player performance. His star pupil has been All-Pro defensive lineman Randy White. From his studies of wing chun, White has learned to instantly sense his opponents' movements, giving him an advantage through the use of his lightninglike reactions. Many opposing coaches have assigned two and sometimes three players to keep White out of their backfield. Ward notes that martial art drills develop sensitivity to initial movement and explosive power to maintain the initiative over the Cowboys' competitors.

Recommended Supplementary Exercises

The Army already uses some fine exercises. Many others have been inaugurated since the Fort Lewis experiments of 1982. The following exercises are meant to supplement these established programs.

Exercises for Flexibility

Some of these can be done by the individual. Others require a partner. Those that involve two people produce bonuses of unit spirit and cohesiveness. These exercises should be incorporated into your daily warm-up and cool-down exercise routines.

Pull forward stretch

Have your partner sit in front of you and press your legs gently out into a seated splits position.

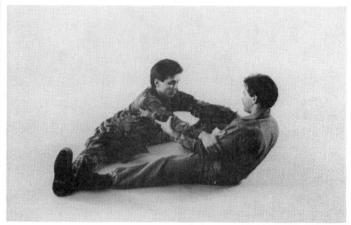

Have your partner gently but firmly pull you as far forward as you can go and hold for ten seconds. Relax back to the starting position. Repeat four more times.

Assisted butterfly

While you sit in the butterfly position, grab your toes and...

Have your partner press your shoulders down firmly and slowly. Do five-ten reps.

Gravity splits

Have your partner get his shoulder under your ankle.

Have him raise up as high as you can **comfortably go** then...

Slowly move back. Stretch each side for 30 **seconds. Do** five reps per side.

Front isometric stretch

1

These are used by Professor Ray Wood at West Point. Have your partner lift your leg as high as it will comfortably go.

2

As your partner holds your foot in place, bear down as hard as you can against his hold for ten seconds. Remember to ease into the contraction.

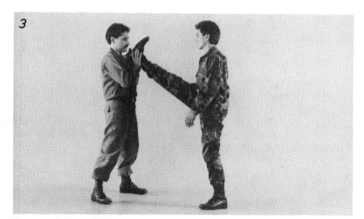

3

Relax and let your partner raise your foot a little higher. In five reps you may get an additional 6-12 inches of motion. Repeat on your other leg. This really stretches the hamstrings.

Side isometric stretch

1

This is like the front version except it is done laterally.

2

It stretches the groin and inner thighs. Do five reps to each side.

These isometrics are the quickest, safest method for producing maximum results. For one of the best sources on martial art stretching, read Bill "Superfoot" Wallace's book, *Dynamic Stretching and Kicking*, Unique Publications, 1982.

Strength and endurance exercises

The following exercises are designed with two purposes in mind. Some give the greatest number of major muscle groups a simultaneous workout. The others produce a maximum workout to isolated muscle groups.

Oriental push-up

These were used by wrestlers in India around the turn of the century in exclusion of almost any other exercise because they affected so many different muscle groups. Although they would execute as many as 1,600 repetitions per day in sets of 100, that is too many for military training purposes. Start with 10-to-20 reps to acquire a feel for their rhythm. Once you have learned the movement, raise your goals to 30-to-100 reps.

Lower your body and move it forward.

Arch your back, stretching forward as far as possible.

Begin with your feet spread wider than shoulder width, your hands on the floor and your buttocks in the air. You should feel a stretch in your hamstrings. If you don't, press back until you do.

Return to the starting position. It helps to yell a repetition count as you thrust forward for each rep.

Manual resistance tricep exercise

These next three exercises are borrowed from Dan Riley's Manual Resistance system. They are great for promoting teamwork within the unit and are a poor man's answer to freeweights.

Stand with your arms down and have your partner hold your wrists.

Raise your arms to the side while your partner resists your movement.

At the top of your motion's range, let your partner reverse his grip so that...

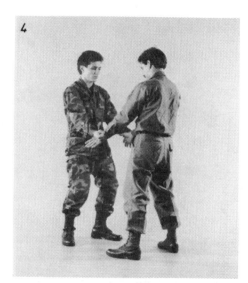

He can give you resistance all the way down. Do at least five repetitions at maximum intensity, gradually building to ten reps. Your partner should resist every movement while allowing you to complete a full motion each way. The same goes for the next two exercises.

Manual resistance curls

Start with your arms down to the front.

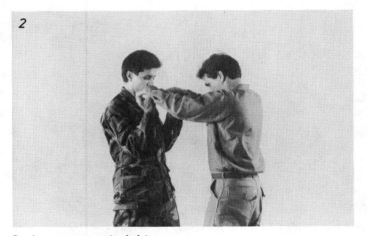

Curl your arms straight up.

At the top of the arc, change grips with your partner for a push-down return.

Manual resistance rows

Straddle your partner and grip his hands.

Pull up your partner's body to your chest.

For one of the best sources on martial art strength-building exercises, read Harry Wong's book, *Dynamic Tension,* Unique Publications, 1980.

Martial Arts Aerobic Exercises

Although nothing beats running for aerobic (car-diovascular) exercise, the martial arts are not without its benefits. During hapkido workouts in Korea, it was common to do 10-to-20 minutes of calisthenics and stretches followed immediately by 30 minutes of kicks. The class then assembled in single file and jogged in place while the first person in line kicked a moving target held by the instructor (a reaction drill). When the first person finished, he went to the end of the line and jogged along with everyone else while the next person in line went through the reaction drills. This would go on for 30-to-45 minutes. You can imagine the fighting endurance and street reactions this kind of exercise produced. The following exercises are good for both aerobics and stretching.

Knee to chest

March in place, bringing your right knee up to touch your chest while pointing your foot down.

Alternate knees. Do 60-120 times per each knee.

Modified running in place

Run in place, bringing your feet up in front of you...

Along the centerline of your body. Keep your knees to the sides. Do 60-120 times.

Martial art Plyometrics

Relatively newly recognized in the conditioning community, plyometric exercises develop explosive power in the legs. They also produce aerobic effects. Some common techniques are high skipping, springing up and down bleacher seats, and bouncing up and down. The following exercises come from judo and hapkido. They are designed to provide the above while developing agility and endurance for combat.

Knee to chest jumps

From a standing position...

Gather yourself and...

Jump straight up, touching your knees to your chest.

Land as softly as possible with your feet widely spread.

Return to the starting position. Do 25-50. Striving for both height and silence makes this an intense exercise in concentration and control.

Knee dips

This can be dangerous so do it on a giving surface such as a mat or sawdust/sand.

Lace your fingers behind your head and kneel, touching one knee to the floor.

Leap high into the air and...

Gently touch the other knee to the floor. Alternate knees back and forth, doing 30-60 reps on each knee. This will very quickly turn your legs into jelly.

CHAPTER 22

Mental/Emotional Conditioning with the Martial Arts

The skill to kill must be matched by a will to kill. Troops must be inured to combat. If not, they may go catatonic or even try to flee. They must understand what closing with an enemy implies and be willing to function appropriately and decisively. Soldiers must also have confidence in themselves and their buddies. The martial arts can be very helpful for this kind of conditioning.

The Fort Lewis Experience Revisited

The High Tech Test Bed (since renamed the Army Developmental Evaluation Agency or ADEA) evaluated the mental/emotional effects of the four different physical conditioning regimens on the test soldiers in addition to the physical conditioning aspects. Subjective questionnaires using the seven degree Lickert scale were administered before and after the ten-week training period. The first area evaluated was the soldiers' levels of self-confidence. The results are as follows:

Mean Group Self-Confidence Scores

Condition	Pretest	Post-test	Change
Standard PT	.224	.402	+.178
Manual Resistance	.412	.428	+.016
CQC/Combatives	.460	.845	+.385
Cbt Obstcl Crs/Run	.169	.275	+.106

Although physical conditioning of any kind tends to boost self-confidence, the martial art regimen produced significantly better results.

Another era evaluated was the military units' morale and cohesion. In other words, what confidence did the participants have in their unit and their buddies? The results are as follows:

Mean Group Unit Morale and Cohesion Scores

Condition	Pretest	Post-test	Change
Standard PT	.307	.503	+.196
Manual Resistance	.628	.592	-.036
CQC/Combatives	.611	.878	+.267
Cbt Obstcl Crs/Run	.258	.360	+.102

Again, the martial arts regimen fared better. Is there any doubt what kind of bang for your buck you'll attain from a martial arts training program?

Instilling Aggressiveness: The West Point Story

The Army's military academy at West Point, N.Y., has a unique problem. It must create competent combat officers out of young men and women fresh from high school. Many of these cadets have never been in a fight. They've never had their noses bloodied or fought despite pain or injury.

Faculty traditionalists require all male cadets to participate in intramural boxing and wrestling. The women are sent straight to Ray Wood's Close Quarters combat course. While the ladies are learning how to make a fist, kick, gouge, scratch and choke, the guys are learning sport art reflexes and rules. Eventually the two tracks come together for one-half a semester under Ray's tutelage. He then has to deprogram the sports reactions out of the guys and ready them for survival on the battlefield.

The method that he uses is unique: He shames them. On the first day of coed classes, Ray has a guy and a girl suit up in body armor, head and face protectors, etc., and tells them to fight. Imagine the guy's surprise when she immediately kicks him in his padded crotch and feints for his eyes. The men are usually thoroughly intimidated by the end of the class period and vow to learn this "dirty fighting" quickly so they won't look like fools in front of the ladies. Ray drives reality home by attacking their most prized possession — their male egos. From that moment, men actively seek to learn combat instincts and aggressiveness. The ladies receive self-confidence in their abilities to fight against men if they have to.

Moral Values and Leadership

Many military leaders are concerned about martial art training. They say, "Now that the troops are all trained killers, what do we do with them? We don't have a war right now. How do we keep them from killing each other or the downtown civilian population?" For these leaders, it should be pointed out that properly taught martial arts programs should include strong doses of ethics and morality, as well as the importance of self-control.

For instance, Ray Wood's West Point program includes that type of instruction and evaluates students for their ethical instincts at the end of the semester. He has devised a martial art equivalent to the police's combat pistol range. Students are run through over 20 grading stations that require them to demonstrate their technical abilities, their aggressiveness, and their ethical judgment under the stress of combat conditions and time constraints. Some stations do not require *any* violence. Students who use it unnecessarily are docked and critiqued.

Killing instincts can be tempered with good sense! The more competent a fighter becomes, the less he has to prove and the less likely he is to misuse his abilities. Deep down, most bullies are cowards. They make up for their lack of self-confidence and self-worth by being aggressive toward weaklings. Once they become competent and gain self-respect, they no longer have a reason to be a bully. Chapter 25 provides a list of ethical rules that should be taught in basic training.

Individual Will — Unit Will

Military units are made up of individuals. How can the unit have a fighting esprit as a team if the individuals don't? Effective fighting units must provide effective mental and emotional conditioning for their soldiers. Combat success does not come cheap. There is no free lunch. After all, the alternative (defeat on the battlefield) makes it all worthwhile. Our soldiers must learn to be gently tough!

CHAPTER 23

Training Facilities and Aids

Martial art training doesn't have to be an expensive proposition. Many military units have the required facilities and training aids already on hand. There are three types of training facilities:

1. Recreation gymnasiums with wrestling or tumbling mats.
2. Outdoor sawdust pits.
3. Any outdoor area picked free of hazardous debris.

Facilities

Almost every Army battalion has a gymnasium with mats. These are excellent facilities for inclement-weather training and for breakfall/throwing practice.

Sawdust pits are cheap and easy to make. Outline the training area of flat, well-drained ground with sandbags stacked one-to-two bags high. Fill in the training area with one-to-two feet of sawdust, which can be purchased cheaply from any saw mill.

Finally, any outdoor area may be used for practice. This is especially important for workouts on uneven terrain. Combat doesn't always happen on nice, flat land. Soldiers must learn to fight effectively on hilly, uneven terrain for realism's sake. "Train as you fight. Fight as you train."

Hilly terrain will cause necessary adjustments to your fighting stances. A low stance provides stability when facing downhill on a steep slope. If you face uphill, you will have to lean into the slope and bend your front leg more. Normal stances are more difficult to maintain on uneven terrain. Kicking while on a slope makes balance rather tricky.

Ground fighting on hills can be very different from an indoor environment. Soldiers need to learn how to use natural obstacles, such as trees, for offensive and defensive purposes. Do not always train on level ground.

Training aids

Make sure to have a number of these training aids on hand. They are easy to acquire and relatively inexpensive.

Wooden knives

You'll need these for both knife fighting and knife defense work. Wood is recommended over rubber because the trainee will get too lax working against a rubber knife. If he makes a mistake against a wooden replica, he'll feel it. Most wooden models are inexpensive and can be found in ads in several martial arts magazines. An even cheaper alternative is to saw off broom handles or dowels in 12-inch lengths.

Focus mitt ($20)

These are used as a target for strikes or kicks. The mitt is used for backfist practice.

Other commercial targets

Canvas air shield ($40): kicks and strikes to the body. Vinyl foam shield ($30): kicks and strikes to the body. Training bags ($60-100): Punch, chop and kicking target.

Homemade hapkido kicking target

This is a very versatile training aid.

It can be used...

For side kicks or roundhouses (or most any other kick for that matter).

Front-kick target.

It can also be used for club defense practice.

How it's made

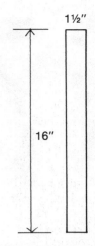

1½″

16″

Cut a piece of one-by-two hardwood 16 inches long for a handle.

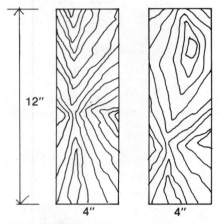

12″

4″   4″

Cut two tread portions approximately 12 inches by 14 inches out of any non-steel-belted tire with a hacksaw.

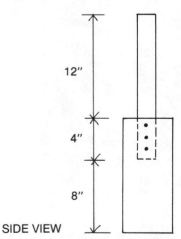

12″

4″

8″

SIDE VIEW

Place the two tire portions with their insides together with four inches of the handle as shown.

END VIEW

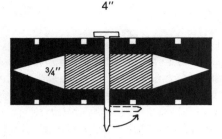

4″

¾″

Nail this together and bend the nails back into the rubber.

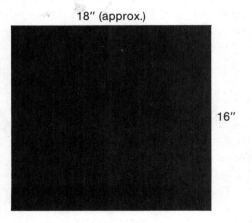

18″ (approx.)

16″

Cut a swatch from an old inner tube about 16 inches wide and long enough to wrap around the rubber tire end two or three times.

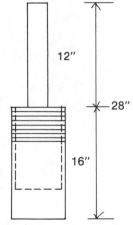

12″

28″

16″

Nail the inner tube on with long roofing nails and bend the protruding nail points back into the rubber. Tape around the nail areas with black electrician's tape. The author's has held up for 12 years and is still going strong.

Whiffle ball bats

These are excellent for club defense practice.

Soft stick

A very cheap and easy training stick or club can be made out of a five-eighths inch wooden dowel rod and the foam insulation sleeves that go over on half-inch water pipes. Cut the wooden dowel to the desired length. Lay it alongside the insulation sleeve and mark off the same length. Cut the sleeve with a sharp knife to length and insert the wooden dowel. If you want to insure that the wood can't come out, put a little wood glue on the dowel before pushing the sleeve onto it. Club defenses and stick fighting can be practiced in relative safety with these aids because they soften the impact of any blows.

Stretching machines

There are several mechanical machines available. The Cadillac of the line is the one that Bill "Superfoot" Wallace endorses. It is expensive ($200-300), but you get what you pay for. They don't come any better. You might consider getting one for the company day room or for the battalion gymnasium. You can order one from: TRECO PRODUCTS, INC., 11846 Tug Boat Ln., Newport News, VA 23606; (800) 368-2224 or in Virginia (804) 873-1177.

Body armor

It's important to use body armor and padding for full-contact free sparring.

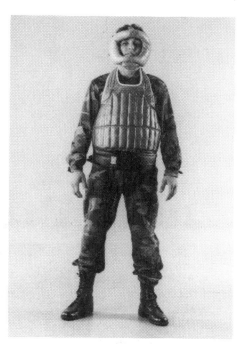

One essential protection is the groin protector. Females should have breast protection. Head and body protection is also useful.

Other body armor is available; however, it is expensive. The above is considered essential. Open-fingered sparring gloves, foot pads, and shin guards are nice to have but are considered optional.

CHAPTER 24

Training Drills

Simply studying techniques can be boring. It's good to use drills that enhance reactions and give the trainees a better feel for battle as a reward or a boredom breaker. There are many inventive things you can do; however, be sure each drill has a purpose and the troops understand that purpose. We already saw how a reaction drill mentioned in the aerobic section of Chapter 21 could be used for teaching reactions and endurance. Here are a few more that you may find helpful.

Dodge the pole

The purpose of this hapkido drill is to develop self-confidence and force-avoidance reactions.

Use a long pole, such as this quarterstaff (Japanese bo), dowel, broomstick, or mop handle. The trainee should stand flat-footed and straight toward the coach.

The coach thrusts the pole forward toward the trainee's torso. The trainee should pivot back and to the side to allow the pole to pass by harmlessly. He should turn his body 90 degrees along with his feet. Execute at slow speeds at first until his confidence is built, then gradually pick up the tempo. Don't let the trainee favor one side over the other. At first have the coach instruct the trainee on which way to spin each time, then let him choose for himself.

Balance sensing

The purpose of this judo drill is to help trainees develop a sense of both their own and their opponents' balance. It allows them to feel the relative and changing balance and body positionings between opponents.

Have each trainee buddy up with another. The relative sizes of each do not matter as long as everyone gets a chance to be with someone his own size, someone smaller, and someone larger.

Each trainee should grasp his opponent's sleeve with his left hand and his opponent's lapel with his right hand (you might want to use field jackets to save wear and tear on the battle-dress uniforms). Have them keep their eyes closed. They should walk each other around a small area so they can get a feel for each other's body movement and balance shifts. Once they have a feeling for these dynamics, they should try to cause their opponents to move further than expected by pulling or pushing (leading their force) his body. They can also sense his direction of movement and attempt to turn it. As one moves, the other may try to harmonize with the movement. If one pushes the other, the pushee may attempt to absorb the movement by standing firm or go force-against-force by pushing back. This is an ideal method to gain an appreciation for Universal Force Dynamics.

Grappling drill

The purpose of this judo and wrestling drill is to accustom the trainees to battle on the ground at close quarters. It also enhances aggressiveness. Pins, chokes, joint locks (not breaks), and nerve pressure-point manipulation are allowed. As a safety precaution, if someone needs to submit, tell him to tap three times on the mat or on his opponent's body. Make sure the opponents honor this by immediately releasing their hold or choke. Standing is not allowed.

Have two trainees sit back to back on a mat or in the sawdust pit. As in the balance sensing drill, mix up the relative sizes of people. This makes it more realistic and pits strength against strength, speed against strength, and knowledge against weight advantage.

At the signal, "Ready, Go!," both should turn toward the other...

And try to obtain an advantage. The winner will be the one who pins his opponent's shoulders down for three seconds or gets him to submit.

Chicken fight

This drill is practiced by soldiers in the South Korean Army. It enhances balance and aggressiveness. It can be used between opponents or in a grand melee of numerous opponents. It is best to have a line of demarcation around the fighting area.

Each person should pick up one of his feet and hold on to it with both hands. Opponents should bang together by hopping one-legged. Whoever lets go with one or both hands or falls down or crosses the demarcation line is eliminated. The last person standing wins.

Free sparring

The purpose of this drill is to develop control and battle reactions in mock battle practice. It is wise to use the protection equipment illustrated in Chapter 23. All trainees should understand the object is not to hurt their partners but to learn from the experience. Force them to go slowly at first so they learn both to develop control and to spot openings. If you see a mistake or a missed opportunity, halt the fight, point it out, and let them continue.

You will find that beginners tend to constantly try to bull their way through their opponents' strongest defenses. Use Universal Force Dynamics terms to suggest other ways of approaching, to attempt feints to create openings, to follow an unsuccessful attack with another that takes advantage of the opponent's blocking motion.

There are many excellent books on free-sparring tactics. Unique Publications distributes many, including:

BOOK	AUTHOR
Strategy in Unarmed Combat	Maslak
What The Masters Know	Maslak
Training and Fighting Skills	Urquidez
American Freestyle Karate: A Guide To Sparring	Anderson
Fighting Strategy: Winning Combinations	Schlesinger
Kicking Strategy: The Art of Korean Sparring	Chong
Tournament Fighting	Vitali
Jeet Kune Do: Entering to Trapping to Grappling	Hartsell
Absorb What is Useful	Inosanto
Hapkido: The Integrated Fighting Art	Spear

One consideration in military free sparring: Don't get carried away with the sport or tournament approach. Remember that you want to inculcate battle reflexes, not "fair target" reflexes. For that reason, allow shots to vulnerable target areas, but only as controlled movements. Stress the golden rule.

An example of why this is important is illustrated by the only two All-Korean Hapkido Free Sparring tournaments ever held. As you now know, hapkido is a street or battle art and not a tournament sport. Unfortunately, participants got carried away with the emotions of competition. The fights became real and resulted in maimings and death. At that point, the Republic of Korea government stepped in and prohibited further national championships in the art.

Don't let your free-sparring sessions get out of control. It's OK to be aggressive, just don't let it get out of hand.

CHAPTER 25

Training Programs

This chapter provides military trainers with a way to organize their training plans in a logical manner. Before starting, it must be said the availability of training hours at the different training schools could only be assumed. Training time availability is a function of program priorities, total time available, and resource affordabilty. The following recommended programs are not locked in concrete. There is no intent to dictate to the military how it must schedule its time.

The ten-hour basic training program

One of the hardest chores for a trainer (or an author) is to select a core of material from a large information pool. If we assume a total training time availability of ten hours during eight weeks of basic training, what selection criteria should we use?

First, recruits need to understand the ethics of what they are about to learn. They must also know their teachers' control signals/measures. Second, they need to learn a foundation of techniques upon which further training programs can be built. The target audience includes at least 10-to-20 percent who have had at least a rudimentary knowledge of the martial arts. A majority of the rest will be anxious to learn. The recommended training subjects should be scheduled as shown in the following training plan.

Related task/conditions/standards are not included since they are a function of training resources and time. Those techniques not taught in the basic program are taught in Advanced Individual Training (AIT) or in the field units.

Ten-hour training plan

Session I Quarter Hour

1. Course introduction and ethics familiarization.
2. Body weapon familiarization.
3. Body weapon familiarization.
4. Stretching exercises (if the troops are already stretched out from other activities, use this time for expanding any weak subject in the session.)
5. Striking familiarization.
6. Striking familiarization.
7. Strike practice.
8. Strike practice.

Session II Quarter Hour

1. Vital target area familiarization.
2. Vital target area familiarization.
3. Stretching exercises.
4. Kick familiarization.
5. Kick familiarization.
6. Kick practice.
7. Kick practice.
8. Review recommended target matrix.

Session III Quarter Hour
1. Stretching exercises.
2. Strike practice.
3. Strike practice.
4. Kick practice.
5. Kick practice.
6. Punch/block familiarization.
7. Punch/block familiarization.
8. Punch/block practice.

Session IV Quarter Hour
1. Stretching exercises.
2. Punch/block practice.
3. Kick/block familiarization.
4. Kick/block familiarization.
5. Kick/block practice.
6. Kick/block practice.
7. Demonstrate the six Universal Force Principles.
8. Provide a Dynamic Factor terms and definitions handout.

Session V Quarter Hour
1. Stretching exercises.
2. Choke/choke defense familiarization.
3. Choke/choke defense familiarization.
4. Choke/choke defense practice.
5. Choke/choke defense practice.
6. Strike/block practice.
7. Kick/block practice.
8. Review course and re-emphasize ethics.

Specific Techniques Selected for the Ten-hour Training Plan

1. **Ethics:**
   A. Never use your skills in anger on a fellow soldier.
   B. Use for defense only, never start a fight.
   C. Select force containment techniques over lethal techniques when not in a battle situation.
   D. Never brag about your skills. You may unnecessarily alert your opponent.
   E. Never deride specific martial arts. They all have strong and weak points.
   F. Never torture or prolong an enemy's pain.
   G. Strive to control or contain your emotions during the fight. Emotions such as fear, hate, or lust get in the way of the battle process. You can let it all go after the battle.

   H. Treat everyone's fighting skills with respect. You never know what your opponent can do. Don't assume an opponent's body structure, looks, weight, or sex will make him an easy win or an unbeatable target.
   I. We take care of our own! Let your buddies know they can depend on you and back it up with action when necessary.

2. **Body weapons:** All of them.

3. **Strikes:** All.

4. **Vital target areas:** All, provide copies of the Recommended Target Matrix.

5. **Kicks:**
   A. Front snap kick.
   B. Low side kick.
   C. Mid-side kick.
   D. Shinbone kick.
   E. Low roundhouse.
   F. Stomp.

6. **Punch blocks:**
   A. Stances.
   B. Avoidance drills.
   C. Deflection blocks.
   D. Arm dislocate.
   E. Sticky-hands jab blocks.
   F. Haymaker elbow lock.
   G. Avoid/Counter.
   H. Deflected body punch.
   I. Uppercut jam.
   J. Backfist block.

7. **Kick blocks:**
   A. Avoidance drills.
   B. Front kick deflection.
   C. Knee kick jam.
   D. Side kick jam.
   E. Side kick scoop.
   F. Side kick deflection.
   G. Low kick avoid and unweight.
   H. Roundhouse kick jam.
   I. Crescent kick jams.

8. **Chokes:**
   A. Bar arm choke from the rear.
   B. Bar arm with neck break.
   C. Rear hanging choke.
   D. Crossed-hands choke.
   E. Bar arm choke from the front.
   F. Side headlock.
   G. Front headlock.

9. **Choke defenses:**
   A. Rear choke defense.
   B. Rear elbow strike.
   C. Front bar choke defenses.
   D. Front hand choke — body weight release.
   E. Side headlock release.
   F. Front headlock release.

The 20-hour Advanced Individual Training (AIT) Program

Although this program would add or replace one-half a man week of training time in AIT, it should be worth it. Remember, it could become a portion of the PT program for which there are already hours allotted. This block of instruction should at least familiarize the soldiers with the basics of battlefield personal combat. Some techniques, especially those from the ten-hour Basic Training block, should be mastered by the end of AIT. The rest will have been learned well enough so that their rough edges can be smoothed in field unit training. Even so, it is impossible to expose soldiers to all techniques in the Basic and AIT time frames. If you find these schedules too ambitious, cut them back to whatever is more manageable and plan on supporting the advanced and sustainment training in the field units with lesson plans, etc.

The 20-hour Advanced Individual Training Sessions

Session I Quarter Hour
1. Review the basic program.
2. Review the basic program.
3. Ethics recapitulation.
4. Stretching exercises.
5. Strike practice.
6. Strike block practice.
7. Advanced kicks familiarization.
8. Advanced kicks practice.
9. Kick/block practice.
10. Kick/block practice.

Session II Quarter Hour
1. Stretching exercises.
2. Breakfall familiarization.
3. Breakfall familiarization.
4. Breakfall practice.
5. Breakfall practice.
6. Strike/block practice.
7. Kick/block practice.
8. Kick/block practice.
9. Choke/choke defense practice.
10. Choke/choke defense practice.

Session III Quarter Hour
1. Stretching exercises.
2. Breakfall practice.
3. Breakfall practice.
4. Throws familiarization.
5. Throws familiarization.
6. Throwing practice.
7. Throwing practice.
8. Throwing practice.
9. Throwing practice.
10. Throwing practice.

Session IV Quarter Hour
1. Stretching exercises.
2. Breakfall practice.
3. Defenses against holds familiarization.
4. Defenses against holds familiarization.
5. Defenses against holds practice.
6. Defenses against holds practice.
7. Ground-fighting familiarization.
8. Ground-fighting practice.
9. Ground-fighting practice.

Session V Quarter Hour
1. Stretching exercise.
2. Strike/block practice.
3. Kick/block practice.
4. Choke/block practice.
5. Throw defense familiarization.
6. Throw defense practice.
7. Defenses against holds practice.
8. Ground-fighting practice.
9. Ground-fighting practice.

Session VI Quarter Hour
1. Stretching exercises.
2. Expedient weapon demonstration.
3. Expedient weapon demonstration.
4. Expedient weapon demonstration.
5. Club defense familiarization.
6. Club defense familiarization.
7. Club defense practice.
8. Club defense practice.
9. Club defense practice.

Session VII Quarter Hour
1. Stretching exercises.
2. Knife-fighting familiarization.
3. Knife-fighting practice.
4. Knife-fighting practice.
5. Bayonet defense familiarization.
6. Bayonet defense familiarization.
7. Bayonet defense practice.
8. Bayonet defense practice.
9. Knife defense familiarization.
10. Knife defense familiarization.
11. Knife defense practice.
12. Knife defense practice.
13. Knife defense practice.
14. Knife defense practice.

Session VIII Quarter Hour
1. Stretching exercises.
2. Sentry neutralization familiarization.
3. Sentry neutralization familiarization.
4. Sentry neutralization practice.
5. Sentry neutralization practice.
6. Lecture and demo on the threat.
7. Lecture and demo on the threat.
8. Review course.
9. Review course.
10. Review course.

Specific Techniques to be Added During the 20-hour AIT Phase

1. **Advanced kicks:**
   A. Back side kick
   B. Mantis kick.
   C. Heel thrust kick.
   D. "J" or scoop kick.

2. **Breakfalls:** All.

3. **Throws:** All.

4. **Defense against holds:**
   A. Rear bear hug escapes:
      (1) Groin attack.
      (2) Foot stomp.
      (3) Head butt.
   B. Front bear hug escapes:
      (1) Ear drum shatter.
      (2) Neck break.
      (3) Groin strike.
      (4) Head butt.
   C. Chest shove counter:

   D. Held wrist escapes:
      (1) Live hand pull-aways.
      (2) Hammerfist escape.
      (3) Cross-wrist lock.
   E. Full nelson escape.
   F. Modified full nelson.

5. **Throw defenses:** All.

6. **Ground fighting:** All.

7. **Club defenses:** All.

8. **Knife fighting:** All.

9. **Bayonet defenses:** All.

10. **Knife defense:** All.

Unit Level Training and Sustainment

The Army's Training and Doctrine Command (TRADOC) does not have the time or resources to teach all the personal combat subjects in basic training or AIT. So, the balance of the subject material must be taught at the unit level. The two greatest constraints are: Who should give the training and when should it be given?

As mentioned in the introduction, many units already have soldiers who are experienced in the martial arts. This talent base should be utilized. The new Physical Fitness Specialist military occupation specialty (MOS) can be found at the battalion level. It should be his job to coordinate such a program, locate the potential instructors from within the subordinates or the local economy, and insure that both PT and personal combat training requirements are met. He should arrange for a minimum of one primary and two assistant instructors for each company-sized training unit.

The easiest time to schedule martial art training is during unit PT time. To insure that the soldiers get PT benefit, stretching and martial art exercises should be scheduled the first 20-to-30 minutes of the training period. During intense training cycles, martial art training should be given three days a week and twice a week in the sustainment phase. Soldiers should stretch and run on the off days for aerobics sustainment.

An excellent way to teach the balance of the techniques is to have some sort of welcome-to-the-unit experience akin to the Ranger Battalions' program. This is a two-to-three-week course in unit traditions, standing operating procedures, and basic soldierly skills. It should be made physically and mentally tough. A martial arts instruction block would be of great worth and would help to establish unit cohesion from the start. At the end of the course, all students should go through a rites-of-passage ceremony to bond them to their unit and to each other. They should be given something to wear as a symbol that they have paid their dues and are now one of the guys. This has been used very successfully in the 9th and 7th Infantry Divisions, as well as in the Rangers. The 101st Airborne Division (Airmobile) has something similar with its Air Assault Qualification Course; however, it doesn't take place at the time a new man arrives. Conducting such a course within a week of a new soldier's arrival goes a long way toward helping him develop a positive attitude from the beginning. It tells the troop his cadre and fellow soldiers really care about him, that they stand behind him 100 percent and expect him to carry his share of the load.

Supplementary Training: Evaluating Off-post Training Resources

Soldiers will read books on subjects they enjoy. Insure that the Post Exchange and local bookstores carry a good selection of martial arts books and magazines. Have your instructors review at least one book every month and provide several copies of the better ones to the day rooms and libraries. Immerse your troops in the Warrior culture and ethic. Bring in well-known martial artists to give seminars and workshops. These people can be identified through martial arts magazines. Frankly, your troops will know who they'd like to hear.

Encourage off-duty participation in martial arts programs. Establish Post-level clubs. Evaluate local available programs. The following are some helpful criteria to use in such an evaluation:

Selection Criteria

1. Do you know anyone currently attending the school? What are his opinions?
2. What are the opinions of students from other schools about the school in question?
3. What is the school's reputation with the local law enforcement agencies?
4. When you observe a class in session:
    A. Is class discipline maintained?
    B. Is a value system taught?
    C. If the instructor has a language problem (i.e., Japanese, Korean or Chinese), does he communicate adequately by some other means?
    D. Is theory explained or is all instruction based on rote memorization and not conducive to easy understanding?
5. Is the school run professionally like a business that is still considerate of the students' needs?
6. Is the training facility kept clean and is its environment conducive to learning?
7. Do you feel comfortable with what is being taught?
8. Are its prices in line with others? If it is more expensive, why is it and is the higher price worth it in terms of added value?

SECTION III
Translating Personal Combat Into Unit Combat And National Imperatives

CHAPTER 26

Using the Martial Arts to Develop Military Tacticians

Introduction

The Army's modern battlefield concepts address the possibility of violent battles fought by forces separated from their parent organizations. These battles may be fought in "islands of conflict" scattered throughout an extensive area. Given the EW, NBC, and space threats, as well as long communications planning ranges, constant communications will be doubtful. The uncertainty of communications raises concerns in the Command and Control (C²) community. As our technological support becomes more complex, many of us tend to assume perfect C² is obtainable and even desirable. With the limitations to communications, perfect, continuous C² will be unlikely.

Perhaps we depend too much on technology. Why is constant command and control necessary? Whatever happened to mission orders and commanders' initiative? Maybe we should concentrate more on the training of our tacticians. In a way, when we say we want perfect C², we are really saying we don't have confidence in our subordinates to perceive the dynamics of the battlefield and to react in consonance with the situation and with the higher headquarter's mission.

Present Tactical Training

This lack of confidence my be engendered by the product of our tactical training system. In the past, the Army has produced tactical geniuses; however, they were either geniuses before they trained or they had a natural talent and were generally exceptional people. The average tactics student became an average tactician. Modern battle requires a great number of above-average tacticians. How do we produce them? To understand our options, let us examine how we teach tactics in the TRADOC system today.

Currently we teach tactical language, formats, and task "laundry" lists. We say we teach a cognitive process when we teach the commander's decision process; however, this is actually another type of laundry list. What we don't teach is an appreciation for force interplay on a personal, instinctive level. We can use tactical exercises without troops (TEWT) to teach an appreciation for terrain analysis; however, there is no violence or anxiety involved and it's usually too time-costly to conduct more than once a course period.

Working with the multiple integrated laser engagement simulation (MILES) system at the High Technology Test Bed at the 9th Infantry Division (Motorized) in 1982, it was noted that squad-sized units required at least three consecutive days and 20 times through an interactive tactical training course before proper tactical instincts were learned and embedded.

At the battalion level, we find the Army's National Training Center at Fort Irwin, Calif., is a valuable experience; however, it is usually a one-time opportunity for most individuals. This means the commander gets a chance to fail the first time through the center, but he doesn't get a chance to reinforce any of his successes. In short, we teach content, but we don't teach the cognitive process well and we don't reinforce positive lessons learned.

Neural Linguistic Programming

To better understand where we may be falling short, let's examine a concept coming from the psychology and counseling fields called neural linguistic programming (NLP). In the mid-1970s, John Grinder and Richard Bandler wrote a fascinating theory in two volumes, *The Structure of Magic (I and II)*. They claimed they had found a common thread among several successful counseling approaches. The most successful counselors all had superb interpersonal communications skills. Grinder and Bandler proceeded to systemize these skills into three modes:

- Visual
- Auditory
- Kinesthetic (body language, physical feeling)

They claimed people use all three modes for communicating; however, they tend to fall back on one as a primary mode under stress. Many even switch from one mode to another depending on the situation.

If we can accept the validity of NLP, we may readily apply it to military instruction. Most of those with instructor experience know a good class presentation should include good visual aids, an effective vocal presentation, and models or actual items for the students to touch, handle and feel. Currently, our tactics instruction relies primarily on visual (maps, printed materials, computer graphics) and auditory (lectures and discussions) modes. We are neglecting the kinesthetic mode. All three modes need to be used together to maximize information flow and understanding.

Kinesthetic Tactical Training

Of what would a kinesthetic methodology for tactical training consist? First we must understand what is being communicated. If the desired outcome is to program instincts for tactics and strategy at an intellectual level, we must consider how they are programmed at the physical level. Tactics is more than an intellectual process (i.e., the Commander's decision process); it is a physical reality. To fully understand a physical concept at an intellectual level, we must first experience it at the physical level. Experience in the Eastern martial arts, Western military/management science, and classic military tactical analysis suggests the possibility that the options for dealing with force in a unit engagement are parallel to those options available in a personal, hand-to-hand combat context. Once personal combat principles become instinctive, they are relatively simple to apply in a unit engagement context.

The Martial Arts as a Kinesthetic Tactical Training Vehicle

The dynamics of the battlefield are easily translated into parallels in personal combat. A good hand-to-hand training program may be used to supplement unit tactical training and to instill tactical instincts. One must caution that such an approach cannot be structured around just any off-the-shelf martial art training program. There are hundreds of different martial art styles. Each one has inherent strengths and weaknesses so there is *no one* correct style.

Instead, the unit's tactics must be examined to determine what specific tactical concepts must be emphasized. Then, parallels from several different martial styles should be tailored to fit the unit level requirements.

To be effective as a training/instructional program, kinesthetic tactical training should satisfy the following criteria:

- Fit within existing class/training schedules to conserve training resources.
- Increase personal skills and self-confidence.
- Enhance unit effectiveness.

Fitting within Schedules

The Army should structure a kinesthetic tactical training program as a supplemental PT program. Most units and facilities schedule physical training one hour a day, five days a week. Most units intensify their program on the first, third, and fifth day with warm-up exercises and a run. The second and fourth days are usually reserved for organized sports. These two days are well-suited for martial arts training.

Increasing Personal Skills and Self-confidence

The bottom line objective is to grow tacticians. As soldiers and officers are trained, they will acquire an appreciation for the dynamics of force on a personal level. If they are taught these concepts by using the conceptual language of unit tactics, they will acquire unit skills much more quickly than previously experienced with the present training system. There are also some interesting side benefits.

A training program such as this had very positive benefits during a High Technology Test Bed evaluation during the summer of 1982. Several physical fitness systems were compared to determine which produced more strength and endurance (push-ups, pull-ups, sit-ups, and the two-mile run), more flexibility (reach beyond toes), greater self-confidence, and greater unit cohesion. Three battalions took part in a comparison of the (a) standard Army PT program; (b) The Pennsylvania State University's "Manual Resistance" strength training system; (c) an obstacle course coupled with a combat cross-country run; and (d) West Point's martial art program. In every event except the push-ups, the martial arts program produced the best results. Probably the most important factor observed during the evaluation was the martial artists' will to compete or excel. The other training participants probably received adequate physical training; however, they didn't try as hard to maximize their test scores like the martial artists.

Enhancing Unit Effectiveness

Raising the confidence and skill levels of individuals in a unit will have a positive effect on the unit as a whole. Soldiers have confidence in their abilities to protect themselves in such units, and they know their fellow soldiers and leaders have the same capabilities. When this mutual sense of competence in self-defense and tactical capabilities is coupled with the belief that "We take care of our own," unit cohesion is greatly enhanced. This was supported by the HTTB evaluations. Soldiers trust tactical competence because it enhances the probability of their personal survival.

The Need for a Common Language

As previously mentioned, unit tactics can be paralleled to personal combat. Likewise, a personal combat concept may be expressed in unit level terms. A common language that bridges the two levels would be very helpful. From this need came UNIVERSAL FORCE DYNAMICS.

The Universality of Force Dynamics

Miyamoto Musashi, Japan's greatest swordsman, born in 1584, killed his first opponent when he was 13. He survived over 60 battles and at least three wars, killing scores of opponents single-handedly. He was known as one of Japan's best masters of the sword and of strategy. His treatise, *A Book of Five Rings,* is the sum of his knowledge on fighting and strategy. It has been applied to life situations and war. This treatise has been used as a model by Japanese strategists in much the same way as Sun-tzu's writings have been used by the Chinese. It is used today by modern Japanese business executives as a basis for corporate strategy. English language translations have become popular among American business executives seeking to better understand their Japanese competitors. It has also been used in the Army's Command and General Staff College for their second-year SAMS students.

If these concepts, based on personal combat, are useful to business, they surely must have application to military tactics study. Musashi's work confirms that force can be physical, mental, emotional or spiritual. It acts and reacts in like manner in any context, be it personal combat, military tactics, personal relations, conflict management, business strategy or government policy. The dynamics of force may be systematically codified into six interacting operational principles and 22 dynamic elements that influence those principles' operations. In Chapter 2, we saw how they can be applied to personal combat. Let's now examine them in a military context. We use them to:
- Deny the enemy opportunities.
- Degrade his operations.
- Disrupt his attacks.

Applying Universal Force Dynamics to Modern Battle

American armies of this century have fought battles much like an American football game. Most campaigns and battles of both world wars, the Korean War, and even the Vietnam War were preceded by a planning phase (much like a huddle). Forces were then arrayed along a forward line of troops (FLOT) or a forward edge of the battle area (FEBA). The FLOT was generally linear in the world wars and in Korea.

In Vietnam, it was frequently circular. In any case, this arraying was equivalent to a line of scrimmage. Action took place with one side or the other initiating the action (taking the offense) and the other side reacting (defending or counterattacking). When the action or play had lost momentum, a lull usually occurred to regroup and to get ready for the next engagement.

The battlefield of the 21st century has different characteristics:

- Large quantities of sophisticated combat systems.
- Difficult command and control.
- No single weapon system will dominate.
- No significant qualitative advantage will be available to the American army.
- Battle will be expanded into the airspace and deep (300 kilometers) into and beyond enemy formations.
- Intensive battles at decisive points.
- Chemical/nuclear/electronic warfare environments.

Tactical situations will be characterized by:

- Decentralized execution by small self-sufficient units.
- Blend of firepower and movement.
- A need to see and strike deep.
- Continuous, as opposed to set piece, operations.

If 20th-century battle could be characterized as being like football, 21st-century battle will be like a hockey game in that it requires:

- Continuous play.
- Plays requiring both teamwork and individual initiative.
- High levels of violence.

This new battle environment could be likened to the mob fights seen in some class B martial arts films. It could also be compared to some of the major Civil War battles of the last century, such as the Battle of Little Round-top, which required combat leaders to create new tactics on the spot.

Such a future battlefield environment requires a different sort of future force epitomized by:

- Small, self-sufficient organizations.
- Highly mobile.
- Firepower intensive.
- Less manpower reliant.
- Extremely agile.
- Capable of fluid, continuous operations.
- Decentralized control.

Such a future force will need new, innovative tactics fought by innovative leaders. These combat commanders and their soldiers will need a new language to describe the dynamic battlefield of tomorrow. Universal Force Dynamics can provide a foundation for tomorrow's tactical concepts. It blends Western world systems science logic with Oriental martial art concepts to attain a simple, yet powerful level of understanding of all forces at play within these complex environments.

The potential effectiveness of Universal Force Dynamics is well-recognized by professional football. Dr. Bob Ward, strength coach of the Dallas Cowboys, is now using the language and concepts of Universal Force Dynamics to teach force and conflict management to the team's linebackers and linemen. Dr. Ward uses these concepts to explain the dynamics of Chinese wing chun and Thai boxing and their application to the conflict strategies on the football field.

Answering the Needs of Modern Battle

Since perfect command and control cannot be assumed on the 21st-century battlefield, we must develop tactical innovators who instinctively understand the dynamics of the battlefield, and who are most likely to select appropriate courses of action as driven by their mission and the battle situation.

Universal Force Dynamics provides a common language and conceptual framework for these future tactical leaders. Tailored martial arts training programs using the language of Universal Force Dynamics can provide the kinesthetic supplemental tactical training methodology to bridge the gap between today's average tacticians and tomorrow's superleaders. This is the kind of trusted training and language needed to promote the type of initiative and innovation in subordinate commanders. Senior commanders must have confidence in their tacticians if power-down leadership is to work.

CHAPTER 27

Universal Force Dynamics in Battle Planning and Execution

The following chapter was contributed by Major (P) David L. Campbell, U.S. Army, military intelligence. At the time this was written, Dave was just finishing a tour as a Threat Instructor in the Department of Tactics, U.S. Army Command and General Staff College, Fort Leavenworth, Kan. Dave had studied hapkido with the author for six months in 1976 when they attended the Military Intelligence Officers Advanced Course together. He has also studied karate. This chapter outlines his perceptions of taking the Universal Force Dynamics (UFD) from the personal combat level and applying it at the tactical, operational, and strategic levels.

UFD and Decisions

The language of Universal Force Dynamics appears to apply to the control and manipulation of force at all levels. As we get to the specifics of how to transition from the personal to unit levels, we can see how forces also operate at levels far above those we normally consider in military units, and in turn, the great influence these major trends have on the way we can operate. Once we understand how these forces are put or not put into motion, we can understand the reason why some simple actions have results which fail miserably one time and succeed with incredible ease other times.

So, let's begin by considering some "truths" about decision-making and UFD, and then examine how we actually tend to make decisions now (not how we

think we make them), and how we can benefit from making our decisions in accordance with UFD principles at all levels.

First, individual and group actions always are made within the influence of other situations and decisions. On the opposite side is the solely human attitude that "What I do counts." Because these two truths are constantly operating, they do influence each other, forming a dynamic process that changes the situation and the content of the next decision.

Second, decisions which are made at one level, "nest" within the situations and decisions made at the next higher level. In most cases, when a decision is made that takes advantage of the situation and decisions at the higher level or lower level, there is an additive effect, or even a multiplicative effect, in the results. If the decision fails to take full advantage of the situation, or acts in the face of the situation, these effects are lessened, or even become a loss.

Third, whatever you do, you may be acting as a tool to accomplish the goals of a higher element. Accordingly, it may be possible for the entire organization to succeed and your portion to fail. The reverse of this is also true, and that potential for both success and failure establishes an incentive for you to do your best. It is, after all, very depressing to those around you when you die, or for you when you do not live up to your expectations. Your feelings on the matter of a personal "terminal failure" are a matter for you to resolve.

Fourth, within the requirements and constraints placed on you by orders and the existing situation, you can develop a unique solution by applying UFD principles to your unit or operation as a whole, or as a mixture of principles. This latter case will work because each subordinate element can use a different principle within its own sphere of responsibility to accomplish your common goal, limited only by the restrictions you place in your own orders to your subordinates and the objective facts of the situation. In these cases, you can work with the aggregated UFD effects of units and weapons systems. You know to expect a certain minimum impact if you employ them in a particular manner on a given mission.

Having emphasized these related facts, we can turn to the transition of decisions from tactical through operational campaigns to the national or strategic level. We will then examine where and how a deliberate application of UFD principles can make an impact at various unit levels.

Operational Decisions

Once decisions are made, organizations and people must determine their specific assignments. The operational orders that come down may spell out particular resource constraints (such as a troop list) or

time (Occupy Obj Alfa by 0900), or they may be more general ("You are to enter the continent of Europe and destroy the Nazi war machine."). Whatever their form, they represent a greatly shortened view of the intentions of the person or group issuing the order. They normally suggest the scope, purpose and limits of an operation or campaign, and whenever possible, they will be accompanied by a written or oral statement of the next higher commander's intent. This statement of intent gives a longer-range perspective for a check against our own plans.

Battles throughout history can be told in UFD terms, although the participants used various terms to describe what they were attempting to accomplish. For example, the Battle of Marathon has the Persians using a force-on-force solution, while the Greeks use a combination of force on force in a deliberately weakened center, leading the Persians into focusing on that weak point, and force turning force on both flanks. As the Persian force began to fall back, the Greeks shifted the focus of their attack and drove the Persians back to their boats (force harmonizing with force). The maneuver was a perfectly executed double envelopment which was aided by the actions of the Persians and resulted in the Greek victory of 490 B.C.

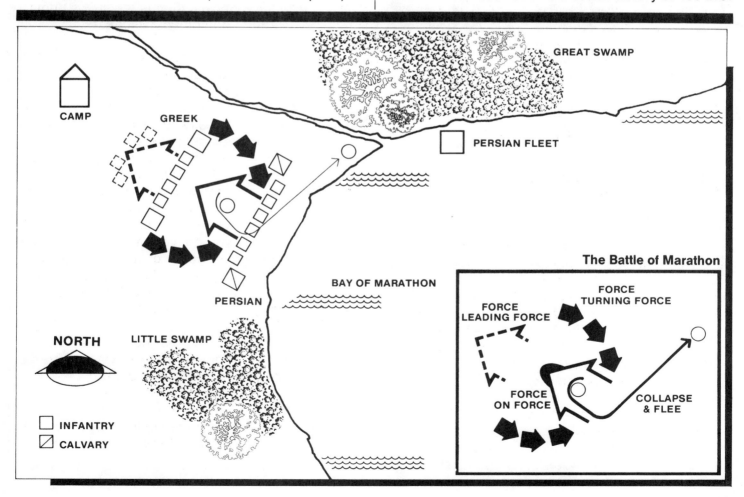

GREAT SWAMP
CAMP
GREEK
PERSIAN FLEET
BAY OF MARATHON
PERSIAN
NORTH
LITTLE SWAMP
☐ INFANTRY
◩ CALVARY

The Battle of Marathon
FORCE LEADING FORCE
FORCE TURNING FORCE
FORCE ON FORCE
COLLAPSE & FLEE

A variation on this theme was played out by Hannibal at the Battle of Cannae in 216 B.C. In this instance, Hannibal arrayed his troops conventionally, and advanced the lightly armed center. As his Carthaginian forces drew back the center, the more heavily armed Roman forces were led (force leading force) deeper into the heart of the Carthaginian defense. As the Romans advanced, they compacted their already-dense formations further in upon themselves, limiting their maneuvering and fighting ability. At last, Hannibal ordered his brother Hasdrubal's cavalry and the heavy wing units of Hannibal's infantry to turn inward (force turning force) to trap the Roman forces completely within the Carthaginian defense. Panic ensued among the Romans and at the end of an additional hour of butchery, nearly 60,000 Roman dead and wounded were lying on the field, nearly ten times the Carthaginian losses.

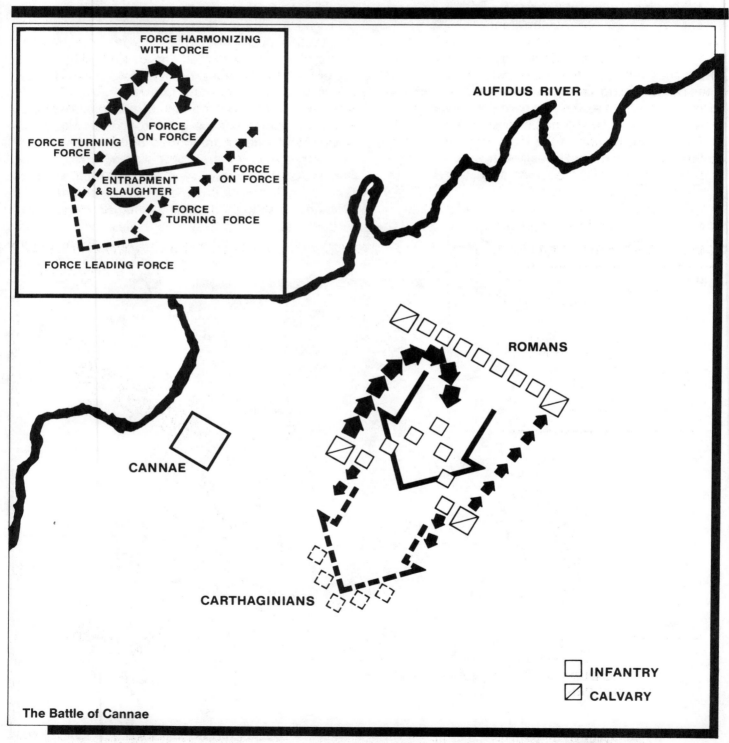

The Battle of Cannae

The Mongol campaign in Hungary, and particularly the Battle of the Sajo River, (Mohi, Hungary) on April 11, 1241, provides an excellent illustration of several UFD principles employed in sequence. In the weeks before this battle, Hungarian forces defended the city of Pest by using the Danube River as a defense line (force absorbing force) while they built their force up to perhaps 100,000 troops. At the beginning of April, these troops marched eastward as some 20,000-30,000 Mongol troops withdrew (force leading force) in front of them. By April 10, the Hungarian forces had seized a bridge across the Sajo River some 100 miles from Pest, expanded a bridgehead and constructed a fortified camp of their wagons to await the resumption of the pursuit the following day. Just before dawn, the bridgehead was attacked and overwhelmed (force on force), permitting the Mongols to stream across the bridge in the direction of the main Hungarian camp. As the Hungarians hastily sallied from the camp to stem the Mongol tide, it became apparent the attack across the bridge was a supporting attack. The main body of Mongols had crossed the river well to the south during the night and now fell on the right flank

and rear of the Hungarian force (force turning force). The Hungarians fell back on their camp and fought bitterly for several hours, finally noticing a gap in the Mongol lines to the west. As the Mongol attack mounted in intensity and the defense began to fail, several Hungarians slipped through the gap to safety. Others followed, and soon a stream of Hungarian forces was flowing through the gap, throwing away weapons and armor (force avoiding force). Having lost all cohesion as a fighting force, the Hungarians were ripe for the final blow. The Mongols, remounted on fresh horses, suddenly appeared on all sides of the fleeing mob and began cutting them down (force harmonizing with force). Within a few hours, between 60,000-70,000 Hungarians lay dead. The Mongols, who had now gained control of all Eastern Europe from the Dneiper to the Oder and from the Baltic Sea to the Danube River, no longer faced any organized forces to resist their planned invasion of Austria, Germany and Italy. Europe was spared that invasion only by the timely death of the Khan and the need for the Mongol generals to return home for the election of their new leader.

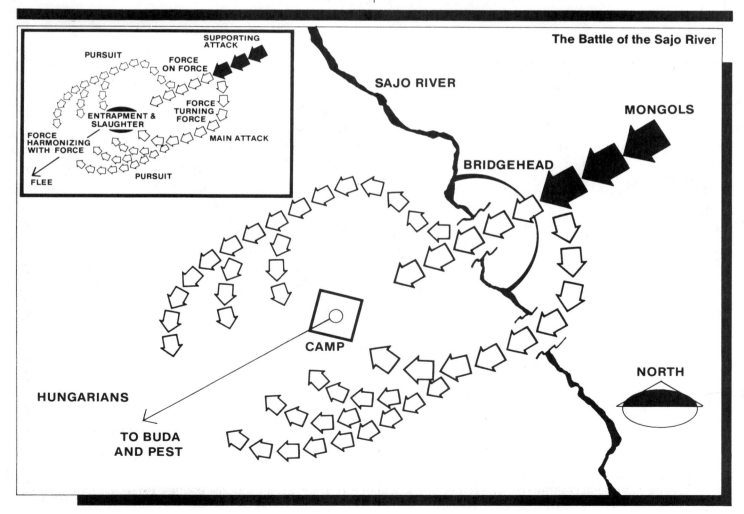

The Battle of the Sajo River

As we will discuss in more detail later, during the British campaign for the Carolinas in the American War of Independence, we note that General Greene's forces were defeated tactically many times but continued to push against the British, finally convincing them that there was no way to retain control of the region. The operational campaign was a success althouç marked by repeated tactical failures. In other situations, such as those experienced by the German force at Stalingrad or by U.S. forces following the Tet offensive in Vietnam, tactical successes were turned into operational failures by strategic "fine tuning."

As a final illustration, let us consider the American Civil War and the often discussed Battle of Gettysburg. Confederate forces repeatedly attempted to advance directly through the Union lines (a force-on-force solution), while awaiting the arrival of an additional crop under Longstreet which would be used to turn the Union left (a force-turning-force solution). In this case, whole corps were committed in frontal attacks, and their divisions and regiments fell as they tried to push to victory. The second-day fight at Little Round-top, which culminated in the famous swinging-door charge of the 20th Infantry Regiment (Maine volunteers) into the flank of units attacking uphill against prepared positions (force turning force on one hand vs. force on force on the other), illustrates two principles in opposition within the context of a single principle being pursued at a higher level of command. The tragedy of the third day at Gettysburg, Pickett's

UFD Factors and Principles of War

UFD FACTOR	Principles of War U.S.	Principles of War USSR	Air/Land Battle Tenets	Air/Land Battle Imperatives	METT-T
Balance		X	X		
Battle/Awareness	X	X			X
Cohesiveness	X	X		X	
Concentration (mass)	X	X		X	
Conservation (economy)	X	X		X	
Coordination (unity)	X	X	X	X	
Deception	X	X		X	
Distance			X		
Effort	X	X		X	
Initiative		X	X	X	X
Maneuver	X	X		X	
Momentum		X			
Position				X	
Security	X	X			
Self-awareness		X		X	X
Situation		X			
Surprise	X	X		X	
Tempo		X		X	
Think/Act thru objective	X	X		X	
Timing	X	X		X	X
Vector	X				
Weapon/Force selection	X	X		X	

(In some cases items marked (X) may be included as a component part of a principle).

Charge, resulted from the continued application of a straightforward force-on-force solution, which was carried forward in the same manner at lower levels. Lee was comfortable with a single solution, and was not inclined to try anything different at that point.

In all these cases, the Universal principles of force dynamics were operating. In those instances where plans deliberately set up a sequence of actions that built upon themselves, the results were extremely rewarding for the victors.

Universal Force Dynamics provides a natural framework for decisions on or off the battlefield. That framework includes and is totally compatible with the principles of war recognized in the East and West, as well as those items now being identified as tenets and imperatives for modern combat at all levels. These factors were introduced and explained earlier in this book. The following table illustrates how these factors compare with the generally recognized principles of war.

On a more personal level, the parallel between repeated frontal attacks and the use of straight punches or kicks is easily seen, and the impact of an unexpected spinning kick or even a hooking punch is easily compared with an unexpected attack from a flank.

Wargame Tactics and Operations

Several years ago, before being assigned to the faculty at the U.S. Army Command and General Staff College, I read an early manuscript on Universal Force Dynamics. For me, it consolidated many differing concepts into a single framework that ran the spectrum of conflict and was not affected by moving across national boundaries and mindsets. In those years it was shared quietly and met with some quiet acceptance. From time to time, it was suggested that the material be prepared as an article for the College Journal, *The Military Review*, and several drafts were actually begun. At the same time, it was felt something more was needed. The opportunity came one fall day when an instructor asked for help setting up a threat attack scenario for a school exercise in the Middle East.

As we discussed the shortcomings of the previous exercise and the additional teaching points we needed to work into the new exercise, we looked at the map assessing the terrain and the entry areas for the U.S. forces. As we discussed the general scenario, I found myself trying to translate the instructor's concepts into the language of UFD, and as I did, I realized the maneuver we were discussing was a two-dimensional overhead view of a double-outside hooking block followed by a front snap kick. In place of my hand movements, I was turning divisions, and in place of a snap kick, I was causing an Army to advance into the gap opened by simultaneous blocks in opposite directions. The next ten minutes were flooded with insight as we looked at each element in more detail, nesting the moves for one level with those of another, building deception plan and real intent on each other, and determining the necessary timing and change in tempo that would cause the maneuver to be a success. Satisfied that we were on the right track, we took our general outline and prepared our campaign outline, specifying the tactical moves and timing that would bring the campaign to a successful conclusion.

Over 3,500 officers faced this campaign in its first three years. One officer in 60 in the first group to face it warned the attack might go as it actually did, but was ignored by his companions. That group went down to defeat, never seeing the real threat until it was too late. The second year, one group recognized the threat, but was too late with its plan. The third year, for the first time, the threat was assessed properly and defeated soundly by one group. In postexercise meetings with the officer students, we described the events they saw using the language of Universal Force Dynamics. In many cases, they started off saying they did not see how or why they were defeated. But when the campaign and deception plan were described in terms of leading, turning or absorbing their forces, comprehension came quickly, and they could discuss their errors of timing, momentum and battle awareness.

I am not ashamed that these officer students failed against our plan. On the contrary. Their failure on an exercise made it possible for them to look critically at what they think they knew about the use of force, and helped them learn the critical principles of Universal Force Dynamics. That knowledge, if coupled with personal practice in any of the martial arts, will place them well on the road to an instinctive understanding of military tactics and operations. That understanding may well be the difference between success and failure at a time when there will be few second chances.

Strategic Operations

Strategic decisions have their beginnings in the existing situations and the influences resulting from the decisions of other nations, the distribution of natural resources, and the expectations and beliefs of people who make up nations and control the use of their resources such as raw materials, production facilities, and transportation facilities for goods, services and information. National leaders envision and enact programs and laws which they believe will be to the benefit of their nations. This results, over time, in new conditions which call for new programs and laws. UFD principles applied at this level might suggest general solutions to problems that would otherwise be overlooked, because the immediate solution is "so obvious."

The key here, as at other levels, is to remember that each sector, and each portion of the sector or organization at your level can apply any one, or more of the principles as an appropriate solution to a problem. And the implementation at the next lowest level may use the same six principles alone or in combination to provide a solution which solves the problem at that level.

So how does this same process apply for military forces at the strategic level? There are many historical illustrations of this process. In the American Revolution, for example, the campaign conducted by the British forces in the Carolinas was faced by American forces under Nathanael Greene. Despite a series of almost unbroken tactical defeats inflicted on the American forces between 1778-1781 (Savannah, Augusta, Charleston, Waxhaw Creek, Guilford Courthouse, Hobkirks Hill, Fort Ninety-six, Eutaw Springs), the British campaign was a failure which culminated in their withdrawal from the Carolinas, a move north to Virginia and subsequent surrender at Yorktown. Greene's campaign had achieved its goal although it could claim but two tactical victories which cost the British about 2,000 dead, wounded and captured. Greene's campaign was one part of a larger national strategy. It took advantage of the unsettled conditions in the South and the extended British lines of communication to convince Generals Clinton and Cornwallis they would be better served by going elsewhere (force absorbing force), ignoring the cold tactical facts that the British were winning their engagements and forcing the Americans from the field or overwhelming them in five out of six contacts (force on force).

A more recent example can be seen in the decision to pursue the Strategic Defense Initiative in the United States. Faced with a large and steadily stronger Communist Bloc, which is motivated by an ideological commitment to spread its version of society worldwide, the United States examined its strengths and limitations and came to several conclusions. First, a situation existed that could not be ignored — that is, a force-avoiding-force solution would only play into a long-term failure. Second, a force-on-force solution was not particularly attractive given the relative sizes of potential belligerent nations, political considerations of allies and our own national consensus, and the potential for continued economic fluctuations and major worldwide loss should direct conflict erupt. Third, a force-harmonizing-with-force solution would allow us to peacefully link a basic shift in defense strategy with the tremendous industrial and technological base available and underutilized in the U.S. and among its allies. Fourth, a force-absorbing-force solution based on peaceful development would be imposed on any group that attempted to match the research, development and production of the U.S. and its allies. The subtlety of this lies in the natural desire to compete and retain what has been developed. The failure to compete would imply acceptance of an inferior status (a matter that is politically unacceptable to the Communist world), while competition would absorb materials, brainpower and funds that would otherwise continue to strengthen its already massive conventional force. Fifth, a force-leading-force solution would set up preconditions for the diversion of additional assets into non-military applications and "spin-offs" such as those which followed worldwide in the wake of the early space programs. This, in turn, lessens the resources which can be committed to maintain and modernize forces at their recent historical rate. It would force a massive, but peaceful research and development contest at the risk of social unrest in the Communist Bloc. And sixth, a force-turning-force solution could be expected to develop with the realization of new capabilities developed by the advanced research and development, possibly resulting in real breakthroughs in science and the development of new systems. If successful, the existing preponderance of forces would be effectively neutralized while the "spin-offs" would continue to stimulate Western economic conditions. In the game of chess, an "elegant move" is one that simultaneously places many valuable pieces of your opponent at risk while blocking any effective response. In this sense, the U.S. Strategic Defense Initiative is an elegant move, utilizing at one time virtually all principles of UFD, and setting the stage for rapid future shifts in operational emphasis.

Dynamic Force Principles Defined

Avoiding Force

General Definition
- Moving out of the way.
- Letting a fist or other physical threat pass by.
- Avoiding dangerous environments.
- Choosing not to compete or confront.

Military Application
- Flanking a superior force, strong point or unit.
- Withdrawal.
- Leap-frogging enemy forces (in airmobile or airborne operations).
- Interdiction fires.

Leading Force

General Definition
- Bringing about a state of imbalance by moving an enemy's force further or faster than he expected it to travel.
- Deceiving an opponent to commit a force in a non-threatening direction or in a wasteful manner.
- Getting someone to waste his time worrying about something unimportant to your true intentions.
- Causing someone to overreact emotionally.
- Drawing out another's true feelings.

Military Application
- Withdrawing, leaving flanks in place to create a bulge.
- Sucking an enemy into an ambush.
- Using a deception operation's real or dummy forces to draw attention to the wrong place.

Turning Force

General Definition
- Changing the direction or vector of a blow or attack. The more force that's involved and committed, the easier it can be to turn, because one's true intention is not readily apparent until it is too late to change its commitment.
- Redirecting one's attention from a true point of concern.
- Getting someone to come around to your point of view.

Military Application
- Rolling up a flank.
- Channelizing forces by using natural or man-made barriers.
- Diverting a force by setting up a strong point like a bunker in their path.

Absorbing Force

General Definition
- Catching, as opposed to blocking, a blow.
- Allowing blows or attacks to fall on well-protected areas until the opponent's energy or resources are dissipated.
- Allowing the force to enter into our area of operations until it reaches its limit of extension.
- Choosing to remain calm in the face of adversity.

Military Application
- Covering force.
- Active defense.
- Superior armor plating.
- Obstacles.
- The use of terrain and vast distances to act as a sponge on the enemy's combat forces as the Russians did to Hitler and Napoleon.
- Force attrition.

Force Against Force

General Definition
- Bringing two forces against one another to one force's detriment.
- Forcefully blocking an oncoming attack or blow.
- Punching through a football scrimmage line.
- Overwhelming with numbers or logic.
- Outshouting someone in an argument.
- Spending more or better time and mental energy in planning and directing an operation against an opponent.

Military Application
- Attack and breakthrough at a weak point.
- Frontal assault.
- Counterattack.

Harmonizing Forces

General Definition
- Coordinating the body and mind.
- Using your opponent's attacking force with your own to defeat him.
- Joining with an opponent to face mutual outside dangers.
- Thinking as your opponent would think to second-guess him.
- Pooling information and resources.

Military Application
- Combined arms teams.
- Turning a unit then attacking in the same direction to change its attack into a rout.
- Pursuit operations.
- Calling a temporary truce to fight a mutual enemy.

The Dynamic Elements of Force

The six principles of force management are accomplished through the use of 22 elements or factors. These factors are interdependent and may be used in many combinations to create opportunities for force management.

Balance

General Definition
- This can include one's personal sense of balance vs. falling. It can also mean the balance of amounts of several forces used simultaneously.
- Holistic, right/left brain integrated thought processes. It can also mean the balance of different levels or directions of thought applied at any one time.

Military Application
- Proper unit mix and positioning.
- Good task force planning.

Battle Awareness

General Definition
- Kinesthetic awareness of the interplay of all forces in a situation.
- Conscious and instinctual awareness of all force within a situation.
- Information data base.

Military Applications
- Good intelligence information collection, processing, and dissemination systems.

Cohesiveness

General Definition
- Sticking to a fight strategy as long as it works.

Military Application
- Conducting operations in accordance with a mission order.

Concentration of Power or Resources

General Definition
- Bringing all power to bear at one place at one point in time.
- Choosing to commit a preponderance of tangible resources to a single choice of alternative actions.
- Bringing one's total mental attention to bear on the job at hand.

Military Application
- Enveloping and penetrating a weak flank with a strong force.
- Using a battery fire of guns simultaneously as opposed to one gun at a time.
- Weighting the main attack.
- Favoring one unit over another for logistics support.

Conservation of Power or Resources

General Definition
- Using just enough material, funds, or strength to accomplish the task at hand.
- Avoiding overkill.
- Varying the mental work to prevent staleness. Not letting conflicting or distracting thoughts drain our mental energies.

Military Applications
- Fire discipline.
- Going to a hit-and-run active defense instead of slugging it out in a static defense.
- Good operations security.

Coordination

General Definition
- Mind/Body integration.
- Fluid, athletic ability.
- Purposing your actions with matching attitudes.

Military Applications
- Proper battle-plan coordination.
- Synchronizing the battle's action.
- Using land/sea/air forces in mutually supporting roles.

Deception

General Definition
- Using feints of the body or head.
- False representations of resources.
- Business misinformation, planned news leaks, or rumors that are designed to mislead.

Military Applications
- Deception operations and feints.
- Psy ops.

Distance

General Definition
- The optimum physical distance between opponents. The degree of relativity between factors of consideration.
- The degree of personal involvement with the situation.

Military Applications
- Distance between units.
- Depth of the battle.
- Range of weapons.
- Communications planning range.

Effort

General Definition
- The amount of physical or material forces being applied.
- The degree of mental energy involved in the situation.

Military Application
- The amount of will and resources committed to the battle. Deciding to commit the reserves.

Initiative

General Definition
- Aggressively beating your opponent to the punch.
- Relying on your own inventiveness.
- Willing to take a risk.

Military Application
- Taking the battle to the enemy.
- Using your own plans as driven by the battle conditions within the context of the mission order.

Maneuver

General Definition
- The ability to move, duck, and dodge to maintain and gain an advantage.

Military Application
- Having the agility to change direction or plans quickly. It denotes quick-minded, flexible leaders and organizations which are able to turn inside the enemy's decision cycle.
- Ascertaining and avoiding enemy strengths while determining and capitalizing on its weaknesses.

Momentum

General Definition
- The moving inertia of maneuver.

Military Applications
- The inertia of the battle. Once moving, the degree of difficulty to stop or change direction or to change plans.

Position

General Definition
- Relative placement of yours and your opponent's body.

Military Application
- Order of battle and forces' locations on the battlefield. This goes beyond the static positions at the start of the battle. It includes the dynamic positional relationships throughout the battle.

Security

General Definition
- Keeping well-protected.

Military Application
- Strong defenses and denying the enemy potentially harmful information (OPSEC).

Self-awareness

General Definition
- Kinesthetic awareness of one's body or organization with its attendant strengths and weaknesses.
- Self-knowledge of one's capabilities, liabilities, biases, and blind spots or scotomas on a real-time basis.

Military Application
- Situation map.
- Operational status reporting systems for:
- Personnel.
- Material.
- Weapon systems and equipment.

Situation

General Definition
- The total fight picture.

Military Application
- The total battle picture and the interplay of all elements and principles.
- The situation drives and tailors most actions in combat.

Surprise

General Definition
- The unexpected or unanticipated use of force or any principle or dynamic element.
- The disruption of the thought process by an unexpected possibility or event.

Military Application
- Surprise is a disruption factor that helps us achieve control or advantage over an enemy.
- Creating the unexpected on the battlefield. This may result from a deception or any unexpected battle opportunity/vulnerability.

Tempo

General Definition
- The rate of physical movement.
- The rate of the thought process.
- Reaction time.

Military Application
- The speed of unit movement and battle flow.

Thinking/Acting through the Objective

General Definition
- Striking through the target.
- Follow-through.
- Carrying the action through, past the logical conclusion or point of impact.
- Pro-action. Planning ahead through alternative possibilities.

Military Application
- Long Range/Plans as opposed to current operations.
- Blowing through primary objectives and going on to secure deeper objectives.
- Interdiction actions.
- Thinking beyond the action at hand to future alternatives.
- Fighting the "deep" battle.

Timing

General Definition
- Insuring force is applied at the proper place and at the proper time in concert with all applicable dynamic elements and principles.
- A sense for temporal reality and dimension.

Military Application
- This is tied in with situation as the fourth dimension of the battlefield.
- First dimension — width.
- Second dimension — depth.
- Third dimension — air.
- Fourth dimension — time (the most critical of the four because it is the most perishable).

Vector

General Definition
- The direction or angle a movement travels.
- The direction or angle a thought or viewpoint comes from or travels to.

Military Application
- Direction of vehicle or unit movement.
- Direction of fire.
- Commander and staff viewpoints of the battlefield.
- Direction of interest (i.e., "Enemy tank at 75 degrees").

Weapon/Force Selection

General Definition
- Applying the proper force with the proper method.
- Choosing the appropriate alternative solution and the proper value system.

Military Application
- Selecting the proper unit or weapon system or type of warfare for the situation.

UNIQUE LITERARY BOOKS OF THE WORLD

Also publishers of:
Inside Karate
Inside Kung-Fu

UNIQUE PUBLICATIONS
4201 Vanowen Place
Burbank, CA 91505

PLEASE WRITE IN
FOR OUR LATEST CATALOG